SUDOKU
CROSSWORDS WORD SEARCHES
LOGIC PUZZLES & SURPRISES!

mind STRETCHERS

VOLUME 9

EDITED BY ALLEN D. BRAGDON

Reader's Digest
New York / Montreal

ISBN 978-1-62145-453-3

Address any comments about *Mind Stretchers, Volume 9* to:

Reader's Digest Adult Trade Books
44 South Broadway
White Plains, NY 10601

Visit us on the Web, in the United States at **rd.com**
and in Canada at **readersdigest.ca**

Printed in China

10 9 8 7 6 5 4 3 2

Contents

Dear Puzzler,

Call me nutty, but having a curious mind, finely tuned by a regular dose of Mind Stretchers, has its distinct advantages.

Of course puzzles bring many benefits such as enhancing cognitive development—making decisions, memory and problem solving.

Puzzles encourage social skills—especially important with younger puzzlers—provoking social interaction when sharing puzzles with others.

Puzzles can teach patience and persistence and other great life skills.

Here is just one example of a puzzle that ticks the social interaction and life skills boxes, but will give you an edge and considerable respect.

Get yourself a bowl containing 80 pistachio nuts. Explain to your unsuspecting opponent that you are to take turns picking up nuts from the heap. You are both allowed to pick up any number of nuts between 1 and 9 inclusive when it is your turn, and you may vary the number each time, if you wish.

The challenge is that you get to pick up the last nut.

There is definitely a way of making sure you always pick up the last nut that we puzzlers can figure out.

Make sure your opponent takes the first pick. Carefully watch how many nuts are picked up. When it is your turn, pick up enough nuts to make a total of 10 nuts for the two of you: So, if he picks up 3, you take 7; if he picks up 6, you pick up 4. Repeat this in every round and you will always have the last pick.

This works with marshmallows, too!

But don't play too many eating games—especially with sugary jelly beans. If you are not diabetic you will soon feel sleepy because your system generates insulin to overcompensate and your blood sugar levels fall. It is because of sugar that insulin levels in your blood surge and your brain is triggered to put the brakes on by issuing a slow-down instruction to the body function department to kick in a "sleep" response.

The theme of the Master Class in this Mind Stretchers issue is "sleep" and in itself sleep is a fascinating subject. Sleep does a lot more than convert the day's accumulation of fatigue into energy.

It has a more specific impact on the knowledge and skills that we have been learning and practicing during the day, or even several days, before. Our bodies may be taking a break, but the brain is accomplishing important work while the body sleeps.

So—on second thought, put the pistachio nuts, marshmallows and jelly beans out of you mind—find that pencil—and settle down to stretch your mind rather than your waistline.

Allen D. Bragdon

Mind Stretchers Puzzle Editor

Meet the Authors

Allen D. Bragdon

Allen describes himself as "the whimsical old dog with puzzle experience and a curious mind." He is a member of the Society for Neuroscience, founding editor of *Games* magazine and editor of the Playspace daily puzzle column, formerly syndicated internationally by *The New York Times*. The author of dozens of books of professional and academic examinations and how-to instructions in practical skills, Allen is also the director of the Brainwaves Center.

PeterFrank

PeterFrank was founded in 2000. It is a partnership between High Performance bvba, owned by Peter De Schepper, and Frank Coussement bvba, owned by Frank Coussement. Together they form a dynamic, full-service content provider specialized in media content.They have more than twenty years of experience in publishing management, art/design and software development for newspapers, consumer magazines, special interest publications and new media.

John M. Samson

John M. Samson is currently editor of Simon & Schuster's *Mega Crossword Series*. His crosswords have appeared on cereal boxes, rock album covers, quilts, jigsaw puzzles, posters, advertisements, newspapers, magazines ... and sides of buildings. John also enjoys painting and writing for the stage and screen.

Sam Bellotto Jr.

Sam Bellotto Jr. has been making puzzles professionally since 1979, when he broke into the business by placing his first sale with *The New York Times Magazine* under then crossword puzzle editor Eugene T. Maleska. Sam has been a regular contributor to Simon & Schuster, *The New York Times*, Random House, and magazines such as *Back Stage*, *Central New York*, *Public Citizen* and *Music Alive!* Bellotto's Rochester, NY-based company, Crossdown, develops word-puzzle computer games and crossword construction software.

When Sam is not puzzling he's out hiking with Petra, his black Labrador dog.

BrainSnack®

The internationally registered trademark BrainSnack® stands for challenging, language-independent, logical puzzles and mind games for kids, young adults and adults. The brand stands for high-quality puzzles. Whether they are made by hand, such as visual puzzles, or generated by a computer, such as sudoku, all puzzles are tested by the target group they are made for before they are made available. In order to guarantee that computer-generated puzzles can actually be solved by humans, BrainSnack® makes programs that only use human logic algorithms.

■ Meet the Puzzles

Mind Stretchers is filled with a delightful mix of classic and new puzzle types. To help you get started, here are instructions, tips and examples for each.

WORD GAMES

Crossword Puzzles

Clues. Clues. Clues.

Clues are the deciding factor that determines crossword-solving difficulty. Many solvers mistakenly think strange and unusual words are what make a puzzle challenging. In reality, crossword constructors generally try to avoid grid esoterica, opting for familiar words and expressions.

For example, here are some actual clues you'll be encountering and their respective difficulty levels:

LEVEL 1   Crichton's *Jurassic* ___
LEVEL 2   Death notice
LEVEL 3   Old money of Rome
LEVEL 4   Living legend
LEVEL 5   Caesarian delivery?

Clues to amuse. Clues to educate. Clues to challenge your mind.

All the clues are there—what's needed now is your answers.

Happy solving!

Word Searches

by PeterFrank

Both kids and grownups love 'em, making word searches one of the most popular types of puzzle. In a word search, the challenge is to find hidden words within a grid of letters. In the typical puzzle, words can be found in vertical columns, horizontal rows or along diagonals, with the letters of the words running either forward or backward. You'll be given a list of words to find. But it does not stop there. There is a hidden message—related to the theme of the word search—in the letters left behind after all of the clues have been found. String together those extra letters, and the message will reveal itself.

Hints: *One of the most reliable and efficient searching methods is to scan each row from top to bottom for the first letter of the word. So if you are looking for "violin," you would look for the letter "v." When you find one, look at all the letters that surround it for the second letter of the word (in this case, "i"). Each time you find a correct two-letter combination (in this case, "vi"), you can then scan either for the correct three-letter combination ("vio") or the whole word.*

Word Sudoku

by PeterFrank

Sudoku puzzles have become hugely popular, and our word sudoku puzzles bring a much-loved challenge to word puzzlers.

The basic sudoku puzzle is a 9 x 9 square grid, split into 9 square regions, each containing 9 cells. You need to complete the grid so that each row, each column and each 3 x 3 frame contains the nine letters from the black box above the grid.

There is always a hidden nine-letter word in the diagonal from top left to bottom right.

EXAMPLE   **SOLUTION**

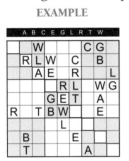

Sudoku

by PeterFrank

The original sudoku number format is amazingly popular the world over due to its simplicity and challenge.

The basic sudoku puzzle is a 9 x 9 square grid, split into 9 square regions, each containing 9 cells. Complete the grid so that each row, each column and each 3 x 3 frame contains every number from 1 to 9.

EXAMPLE   **SOLUTION**

As well as classic sudoku puzzles, you'll also find sudoku X puzzles, where the main diagonals must also include every number from 1 to 9, and sudoku twins with two overlapping grids.

Kakuro

by PeterFrank

These puzzles are like crosswords with numbers. There are clues across and down, but the clues are numbers. The solution is a sum which adds up to the clue number.

Each number in a black area is the sum of the numbers that you have to enter in the empty boxes beside or below. The empty boxes that make up the sum are called a run. The sum of the across run is written above the diagonal in the black area, while the sum of the down run is written below the diagonal.

Runs can contain only the numbers 1 through 9, and each number in a run can only be used once. The gray boxes contain only odd numbers and the white contain only even numbers.

EXAMPLE   **SOLUTION**

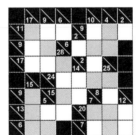 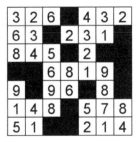

Binairo

by PeterFrank

Binairo puzzles look similar to sudoku puzzles. They are just as simple and challenging but that is where the similarity ends.

There are two versions: odd and even. The even puzzles feature a 12 x 12 grid. You need to complete the grid with zeros and ones, until there are 6 zeros and 6 ones in every row and every column. No more than two of the same number can be next to or under each other. Rows or columns with exactly the same combination are not allowed.

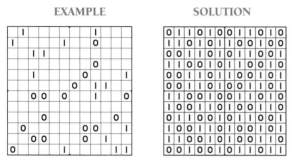

EXAMPLE	SOLUTION

The odd puzzles feature an 11 x 11 grid. You need to complete the grid with zeros and ones until there are 5 zeros and 6 ones in every row and column.

Keep Going

In this puzzle, start on a blank square of your choice and connect as many blank squares as possible with one single continuous line.

You can only connect squares along vertical and horizontal lines, not along diagonals. You must continue the connecting line up until the next obstacle—i.e., the rim of the box, a black square or a square that has already been used.

You can change direction at any obstacle you meet. Each square can only be used once. The number of blank squares left unused is marked in the upper square. There is more than one solution, but we only include one solution in our answer key.

EXAMPLE
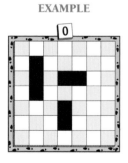

SOLUTION
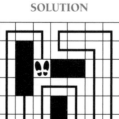

Number Cluster
by PeterFrank

Number Cluster puzzles are language-free, logical numerical problems. They consist of cubes on a 6 x 6 grid. Numbers have been placed in some of the cubes, while the rest are empty. Your challenge is to complete the grid by creating runs of the same number and length as the number supplied. So where a cube with the number 5 has been included on the grid, you need to create a run of five number 5's, including the cube already shown. The run can be horizontal, vertical, or both horizontal and vertical.

EXAMPLE　　SOLUTION

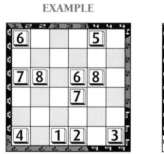

Word Pyramid

Each word in the pyramid has the letters of the word above it, plus a new letter.

Start with the answer to No.1 and work your way to the base of the pyramid to complete the word pyramid.

Sport Maze

This puzzle is presented on a 6 x 6 grid. Your starting point is indicated by a red cell with a ball and a number. Your objective is to draw the shortest route from the ball to the goal, the only square without a number. You can only move along vertical and horizontal lines, but not along diagonals. The figure on each square indicates the number of squares the ball must be moved in the same direction. You can change direction at each stop.

EXAMPLE	SOLUTION

Cage the Animals

This puzzle presents you with a zoo divided into a 16 x 16 grid. The different animals on the grid need to be separated. Draw lines that will completely divide up the grid into smaller squares, with exactly one animal per square. The squares should not overlap.

EXAMPLE	SOLUTION

VISUAL PUZZLES

Throughout *Mind Stretchers* you will find unique mazes, visual conundrums and other colorful challenges. Each comes with a new name and unique instructions. Our best advice? Patience and perseverance. Your eyes will need time to unravel the visual secrets.

BrainSnack® Puzzles

To solve a BrainSnack® puzzle, you must think logically. You'll need to use one or several strategies to detect direction, differences and/or similarities, associations, calculations, order, spatial insight, colors, quantities and distances. A BrainSnack® ensures that all the brain's capacities are fully engaged. These are brain sports at their best!

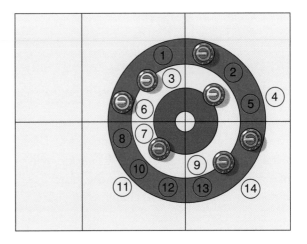

Sunny Weather

We all want to know the weather forecast, and here's your chance to figure it out! Arrows are scattered on a grid. Each arrow points toward a space where a sun symbol should be, but the symbols cannot be next to each other vertically, horizontally or diagonally. A symbol cannot be placed on top of an arrow. You must determine where the symbols should be placed.

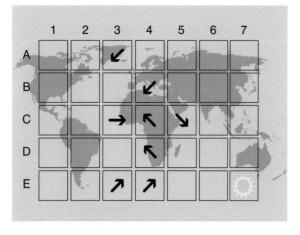

BRAIN TEASERS

You'll also find more than 100 short brain teasers scattered throughout these pages. These puzzles, found at the bottom of the page, will give you a little light relief from the more intense puzzles while still challenging you.

• ONE LETTER LESS OR MORE

A G E N C I E S ⊖ E ☐ ☐ A ☐ ☐ ☐

• LETTERBLOCKS

• BLOCK ANAGRAM

SHADY OIL   (leisure time away from work)

☐ ☐ ☐ ☐ ☐ **A** ☐ ☐

• DOODLE PUZZLE

• SQUIRCLES

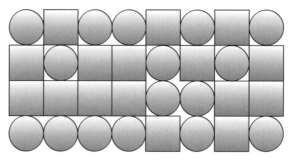

But wait—there's more!

There are additional brain teasers at the top of odd numbered pages, organized into two categories:

• **QUICK!:** These tests challenge your ability to instantly calculate numbers or recall well-known facts.

• **DO YOU KNOW...:** These more demanding questions probe the depth of your knowledge of facts and trivia.

■ Master Class:

Sshh! Do Not Disturb!

Thomas Edison reputedly had little patience for sleep. It's no coincidence that Edison labored hard to develop practical forms of electrical lighting, so people could do something useful at night instead of squinting by candle or lying in the darkness like hibernating animals.

Workaholics like Edison bemoan the fact that a third of their life is spent in apparent idleness. (Actually, Edison claimed to sleep only four hours a night. More on that later.) Just think how much more they could accomplish if they didn't have to sleep at all!

Modern Researchers Don't Agree That Sleep Is Wasted Time

If Edison had invented a good brain imaging machine instead of an incandescent light bulb, he might have realized that sleep isn't something that gets in the way of productivity. In fact, according to a burgeoning body of evidence, it plays a crucial complementary role to the busy waking state that Edison wished to maximize.

In sleep, we reinforce knowledge picked up while we were awake, so that we remember it better. Both states work together to foster learning and invention.

How Sleep Is Essential to Cognition as a Practical Matter

What are the limits to the kinds of learning that a night's sleep can help you accomplish? Is sleep important for abstract, conceptually challenging learning processes such as developing and retaining a detailed understanding of, say, Constitutional law? Or is it just used in consolidating knowledge of simpler things like the route to work or a good tennis swing?

Nobody really knows the answer to that yet. Most of the carefully controlled experiments with humans have involved relatively simple, easily quantified tasks such as the kinds of spatial memory and motor skills just mentioned.

Sleep Consolidates Language Learning

Basic language tasks, such as memorizing lists of words, have been tested for effects of sleep. An experiment reported not too long ago in the journal *Nature* offers evidence that sleep is used to consolidate more complex kinds of linguistic knowledge in addition to rote learning.

In the experiment, researchers trained subjects to recognize words generated by a speech synthesizer, a surprisingly challenging task that can take months to perfect. After a morning study session, the subjects' recognition skills declined over the course of the day, but rebounded after a night's sleep—the typical kind of effect that sleep has on other learning tasks as well.

It wasn't a process of rote learning, because what was required was an ability to generalize across a range of acoustic patterns rather than just memorizing specific words. This is the same skill used in natural language processing when we learn to count two instances of a phoneme such as "t" as the same sound even though they are acoustically different from one word to the next, or from one speaker to the next. Say these words out loud and listen to the different ways you pronounce the "t": ten, stop, pit, butter, button. Or think of the kind of adjustment you have to make when listening to someone who speaks with an accent. In *My Fair Lady*, Eliza Doolittle pronounced "Spain" the way you might pronounce "spine," yet you were able to make the mental adjustment necessary to understand what she was saying.

No Evidence for Learning From a Tape While Sleeping

The fact that your sleeping brain may be working on language tasks should not, however, be understood to mean that you might benefit from playing language tapes while you sleep. There is no good evidence that your sleeping brain processes incoming data of that sort in any way that would let you learn it. The important work the brain performs while you sleep is off-line, done while it is shut off from external sensory input.

So you'd be better off saving your money for a good mattress.

How Much Sleep Do You Need?

An emerging view of sleep and learning is that it's important to sleep long enough for the brain to go through at least a few cycles of Rapid Eye Movement (REM) sleep—the phase in which we usually dream—and non-REM sleep characterized by slower wavelengths of electrical activity. Those different sleep stages may have a relationship to one another that is analogous to the relationship between sleeping and waking: it's not that one is important and the other unimportant, both are essential complementary parts of a whole.

During slow-wave sleep the brain sorts through the day's experiences and decides which to remember. Then, when the brain enters the REM stage of the sleep cycle, it is strengthening the neural connections underlying that new knowledge.

We experience that process as dreaming.

At Least Six Hours of Sleep Takes Advantage of the Brain's System to Help Learning

The usual advice is to sleep about eight hours a night. Of course, everybody is different—some people need more sleep than this; some people need less. Edison, assuming he really did get just four hours of sleep a night, may just have been at the low end of the range. Some research does support the idea that successful "short sleepers"—like Edison—tend to spend a somewhat higher proportion of their sleep in the REM and slow-wave states, thus efficiently maximizing their beneficial effects.

Sleeping on the Job

Recent studies confirm that a brief midday sleep can have a restorative effect on the brain's learning mechanism, reversing the kind of deterioration that tends to occur over the course of a day. How long a nap works best?

A Harvard study, reported in *Nature Neuroscience*, found that a one-hour nap in the early afternoon had a better effect than a half-hour nap. Not coincidentally, perhaps, only the one-hour nap was long enough to show the same mix of REM and non-REM sleep typically found in a longer nighttime slumber.

If Your Brain Is Like a Saturated Sponge, a Nap Can Wring It Out

Practicing a new skill repeatedly over the course of a day appears to have an effect like gradually filling a sponge with water. The sponge absorbs more and more water up to the point of saturation. A nap has the effect of wringing the water out of the sponge to allow it to absorb more. In this analogy, the process of wringing out the sponge is a process of retaining information, not discarding it. If water is squeezed out of the sponge into a bucket, think of the bucket as the brain's long-term memory store.

In fact, imagine that your brain has different sponges for mopping up different things. If you can't nap but you switch to a different task, your brain will regain its learning curve. Like napping, alternating tasks can aid the process of learning them.

A Brain Exercise: The Logic of Dreams

How do you know your entire life isn't a dream dreamed by a creature about to wake up? You don't. The best René Descartes could conclude was this:

The fact that I am thinking must mean that there is a thinker of some sort behind my thoughts—"I think, therefore I am." But what am I? There's no way to know for sure.

Imagine there's a land called Dreamland where everybody is one of two types: diurnal (active by day) and nocturnal (active by night). Everything that a diurnal person believes while he is awake is true, while everything he believes while asleep is false.

For nocturnal people, everything is just the opposite. What they believe while asleep is true; everything they believe while awake is false.

OK so far? The following Dreamland questions (inspired by the "Isle of Dreams" chapter of Raymond Smullyan's *The Lady or the Tiger*) are ranked in order of increasing difficulty.

First question
One of the inhabitants of Dreamland believed he was asleep.
What type was he?

Second question
Another inhabitant, at some time, believed he was asleep and diurnal.
Was he awake or asleep?

Third question
Another inhabitant believed that both he and his sister were nocturnal. At the same time, his sister believed that he was not nocturnal.
Was he nocturnal or diurnal?
How about his sister? Was he awake or asleep?

Answers are at the end of this Master Class. (Drawing a grid may help keep track of the possibilities.)

Do all animals...

... sleep? As far as we know, yes. The amount of time spent sleeping varies dramatically from one animal to the next. A giraffe sleeps a total of only about 2 hours in each 24-hour cycle. A python sleeps about 18. Cats? About 12. Elephants? 4. A human infant sleeps twice as many hours (16) as an adult. Dolphins sleep with only one hemisphere of their brain in slow-wave sleep at a time.

... dream? Almost all mammals and birds experience brain activity during sleep that seems to correspond to the human REM state. The only exception thus far discovered is the echidna, a hedgehog-sized anteater native to Australia and New Guinea.

By using computer mapping and recording electrical brain activity, researchers discovered that a little bird called the zebra finch is capable of learning new songs while it sleeps.

Mapping Music in the Mind

This hardy finch, native to Australia, can be found in pet stores and in biology labs where the males have been extensively studied for their bird-song behavior (the male finch must sing to attract a mate). A structure in the finch forebrain called the RA (*robustus archistriatalis*) is involved in processing and producing songs. Scientists Dr. Zhiyi Chi and Dr. Daniel Margoliash from the University of Chicago measured and mapped the electrical activity of RA neurons while the finch was awake and singing, and then again, while the finch slept. Results? Neurons fired in complex patterns while the bird was singing, but interestingly, these same patterns fired while the bird slept, although no sound was being produced. Even more astounding is that new patterns were recorded while the bird slept, and these new patterns were later repeated upon awakening when the bird sang new, previously unheard songs.

It appears that during sleep, finches are not only capable of replaying and rehearsing songs they already know, but can create, record and replay new songs in their heads. "From our data we suspect the songbird dreams of singing," says Dr. Margoliash. "The zebra finch appears to store the neuronal firing pattern of song production during the day and reads it out at night, rehearsing the song and, perhaps, improvising variations. The match is remarkably good."

Human Translation

Because the zebra finch goes through the same stages of sleep as mammals do, studying this bird's remarkable sleeping-brain ability may explain how humans learn language, or help treat certain speech and learning disorders, or even lead to ways people can practice, learn or create during sleep.

As an endnote, there are some musicians—Sting, Billy Joel, Paul McCartney—who claim they have created songs in their sleep. In fact, one of the most recorded songs in history, *Yesterday* by Paul McCartney is a melody that came to the former Beatle in a dream.

Answers to the Dreamland questions:
First question
He was nocturnal. If he were diurnal and he was awake, he would believe he was awake. If he were diurnal and he was asleep, he would believe he was awake. If he were nocturnal, he would believe he was asleep whether he was asleep or not.
Second question
He was awake, and he was nocturnal. Therefore his belief was false.
Third question
He was nocturnal, he was awake, and his sister was diurnal.

Allen D. Bragdon

★ Fruit Punch by Michele Sayer

ACROSS

1 Rotisserie part
5 Pinheads
10 Gambol
14 Verdi opera
15 Acclimatize
16 Toledo's lake
17 Desire
18 Extortionist, e.g.
19 Ashen
20 Florida's spring training league
22 By and by
23 Horatian poems
24 Beatnik's "Got ya!"
26 *The Mask of Dimitrios* novelist
29 Franklin bills
33 Nancy of *Baywatch*
34 Stephen King's *Bag of ___*
35 Marceau character
36 Duck genus
37 Calyx part
38 Fashion designer Chanel
39 Nero's 98
40 Hectare's 2.47
41 Self-help book genre
42 Resort ENE of Tampa
44 Dickie feature
45 "Madcap Maxie" of boxing
46 Frigophobiac's fear
47 Hasn't ___ to stand on
49 Select carefully
55 *Rubber Soul* tune
56 Itchy
57 Petty in *Free Willy*
58 French 101 verb
59 Petting zoo favorite
60 Missing, militarily
61 During working hours
62 Alpine air
63 Real bore

DOWN

1 Did karaoke
2 Anchorage
3 Fresh thought
4 They croak when they get older
5 Don't agree
6 Extraordinary people
7 Ripsnorter
8 *Star Trek: TNG* empath
9 Lookout
10 Restore
11 Miami stadium
12 O'Shea in *Ulysses*
13 Ball-___ hammer
21 First lady's garden
25 Dentist
26 Be of value to
27 Fad
28 RIM smartphone

29 Had fingers crossed
30 Some, in Spain
31 Formal fiats
32 Animal's track
34 Swiss capital
37 Barely
38 "Clocks" group
40 Pub pint
41 Pious
43 "Hotel California" group
44 Ranch enclosure
46 ___ de menthe
47 On in years
48 Ford of The Runaways
50 Angelic circle
51 "Good grief!"
52 *The Music Man* setting
53 Grammy winner Sheryl
54 Potter's oven

★★ Number Cluster

Complete the grid by constituting adjoining clusters that consist of as many cubes as the number on the cubes. At cube 5, for instance, you will have to make a five-cube cluster. Two or more figure cubes of the same value belong to the same cluster. You can only place your cubes along horizontal and/or vertical lines.

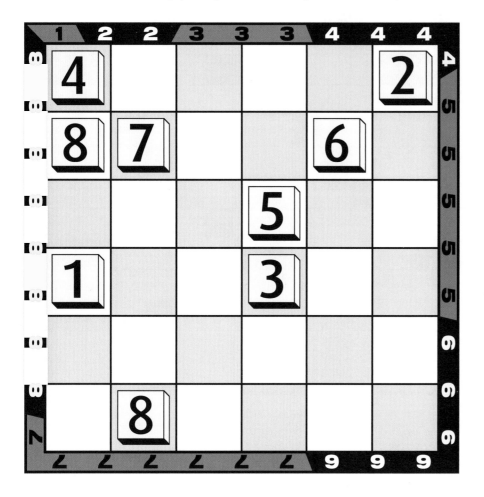

ONE LETTER LESS OR MORE

The word on the right side contains the letters of the word on the left side plus or minus the letter in the middle. One letter is already in the right place.

A L P I N I S T -L   A

★ BrainSnack®—Jump to It

Which number should replace the question mark?

UNCANNY TURN

Rearrange the letters of the word below to form a cognate anagram, one which is related or connected in meaning to the original phrase. The answer can be one or more words.

BASIC

★ ABBA Hits by John McCarthy

ACROSS

1 Saw or wind ender
5 Go over big
10 Fish bait
14 Charles Lamb's nom de plume
15 Crow toe
16 Mrs. Charlie Chaplin
17 Sty cry
18 Christensen in *Traffic*
19 Perturbed state
20 ABBA song
22 Choral pieces
24 Action break
25 Currently
26 Plaza de la Revolución setting
29 Suffering
32 Stratosphere layer
33 Biospheres
34 Start of a series
35 Casino game
36 Having two feet
37 Cost of cards
38 "___ Blu Dipinto di Blu"
39 Makeup tool
40 Use a prayer rug
41 Canadian Arctic sights
43 Woodland gods
44 Hot, in a way
45 Feel
46 Like Oscar Night parties
48 ABBA song
52 Black, to bards
53 Immerse
55 Fork-tailed gull
56 Nickname for a slow person
57 Symbol on a one-way sign
58 Stonestreet of *Modern Family*
59 Cher's *Burlesque* role
60 Boxers' cries
61 1948 Hitchcock film

DOWN

1 *Cats* noise
2 Skating star Kulik
3 Scurge of serge
4 City between Tampa and Orlando
5 Designer McCartney
6 December air
7 Mingle-mangle
8 *M*A*S*H* soldier
9 Bewitched
10 *Fair Ball* author Bob
11 ABBA song
12 Component
13 Yoga class supplies
21 Mystic letter
23 They may be set in Vegas
25 Less likely to bite
26 Ex-Egyptian president Mubarak

27 Montezuma, for one
28 ABBA song
29 Expectations
30 Bury
31 Takes it all off
33 Dreary
36 Special occasion
37 Aardvark
39 Without
40 Madeline in *Blazing Saddles*
42 Creatures
43 Threaded fasteners
45 Phrygian fabulist
46 "___ we forget ..."
47 Proficient
48 Secure a flag
49 Roman emperor
50 Leaky faucet sound
51 Formerly
54 Hematite, e.g.

★ Verbs

All the words are hidden vertically, horizontally or diagonally—in both directions. The letters that remain unused form a sentence from left to right.

```
A Y C R E A K V R E R R B P E
T L A O N G E K T E E H U Z E
R L M E D W I T N G P Y E T H
E U O X O R I T G I D E I S E
N B U E R S I A U I R N A G X
E B F C S J T L T F K H A T A
R E L U E S C E L L D R S P M
V C A T T A A A E N D R A D I
A P G E L O T R S E S N I I N
T B E V L S Y N N A I M D N E
E E E I A R E C T C O A B J K
E M C O T F C I S U M E K A M
O U B N E T S I L R P R M M D
W S S T C H E E R H O D L N E
H N J A B B E R B A H S I I S
I O N I A L P M O C S B F O F
Z C I G A M O D E L B M U R G
Z A S E C L I M B N T E N C E
```

DRILL
DRINK
ENDORSE
ENERVATE
EXAMINE
EXECUTE
FILM
FREEZE
GARDEN
GRUMBLE
JABBER
LEARN
LISTEN
MAKE MUSIC
PANIC
REPEAT
SHOP
SHRINK
STAGGER
TIDY UP
TINKLE
WHIZZ

BIND
BOAST
BULLY
CALVE

CAMOUFLAGE
CHEER
CLIMB
COMPLAIN

CONSUME
CREAK
DO MAGIC
DREAM

CHANGE ONE

Change one letter in each of these two words to form a common two-word phrase.

CROP CUT

★★ Keep Going

Start on a blank square of your choice and connect as many blank squares as
possible with one single continuous line. You can only connect squares along
vertical and horizontal lines, not along diagonal lines. You must continue the
connecting line up until the next obstacle, i.e., the rim of the box, a black
square or a square that has already been used. You can change direction at any
obstacle you meet. Each square can only be used once. The number of blank
squares that will be left unused is marked in the upper square. There is more
than one solution. We only show one solution.

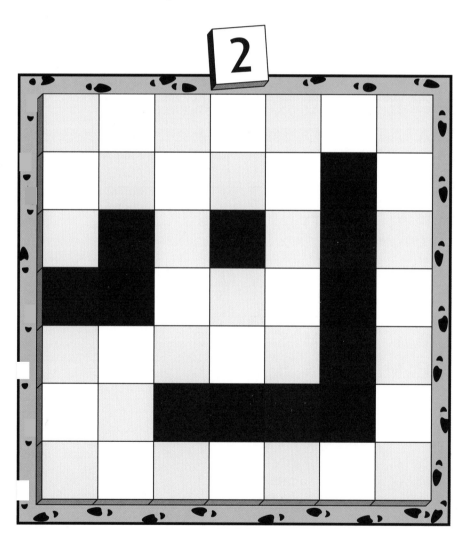

FRIENDS

What do the following words have in common?

WEAPON CALENDAR STORE TANKER VISOR INFECTION

★ Popular Pets by Karen Peterson

ACROSS

1 Free ticket
5 Organ features
10 *Lost Horizon* guru
14 Bose of Bose Corp.
15 "___ Was a Lady" (1932 song)
16 Plane designer Sikorsky
17 Peace Nobelist Eisaku
18 Virgo's alpha star
19 Jockey's whip
20 Dr. Seuss book
23 At a previous time
24 Be obliged to
25 Picnic pest
26 Friml's *Donkey* ___
31 Moon's path
34 School group
35 Dirty double-crosser
36 Organic soil
37 Quit
38 Building by a barn
39 Alpine river
40 Miss Hawkins of Dogpatch
41 Lover boy
42 Scare
44 ___ *Mir Bist Du Schoen*
45 "Fat chance!"
46 Don
50 Ouida story
54 God or asteroid
55 Fragrant spring shrub
56 Made an advance
57 Blowgun ammo
58 River from the Savoy Alps
59 Irish language
60 BPOE members
61 Perk up
62 Neural network

DOWN

1 Hindu social class
2 City in Nebraska
3 Alma ___
4 Herald
5 Poem of six lines
6 Swinelike animal
7 Asgard god
8 Early Briton
9 Aquarium favorite
10 Moss
11 Indian tourist town
12 Disputable
13 Dada artist
21 "It ___ Necessarily So"
22 Mama llamas
26 Done in
27 Bed of roses
28 Covent Garden solo
29 Spanish surrealist
30 Town on the Thames
31 *Lemony Snicket* villain
32 Greeting from Simba
33 Naples neighbor
34 Give up land
37 Holy See religion
38 Ponzi schemer
40 Rug type
41 Penn in *Milk*
43 Pac-Man chasers
44 Stiff drink
46 Harsh light
47 Tractor name
48 Blofeld of Bond films
49 Perfumer Lauder
50 Asia's shrinking sea
51 Blockhead
52 Go angling
53 Skip town
54 Dutch city

★★★ Sudoku

Fill in the grid so that each row, each column and each 3 x 3 frame contains every number from 1 to 9.

	1				9	7	4	2
7	4					8	6	5
	2				7	3	1	9
5	8			7				
				2	8	5		1
9	7	1	3					
	3		1					8
			6				5	
						6		

DOODLE PUZZLE

A doodle puzzle is a combination of images, letters and/or numbers that represent a word or a concept. If you cannot solve a doodle puzzle, do not look at the answer right away. Think hard—and outside the box.

TIME

★★★ Sport Maze

Draw the shortest way from the ball to the goal. You can only move along vertical and horizontal lines, not along diagonal lines. The figure on each square indicates the number of squares the ball must be moved in the same direction. You can change direction at each stop.

3	2	4	4	4	4
2	3	1	2	3	5
2	1	0	1	2	1
4	4	3	3	3	4
1	3	4	1	2	1
2		1	5	5	2

ONE LETTER LESS OR MORE

The word on the right side contains the letters of the word on the left side plus or minus the letter in the middle. One letter is already in the right place.

B A C T E R I A -I ☐ ☐ ☐ A ☐ ☐ ☐

★ Checkmate! by John M. Samson

ACROSS

1 Tabby's call
5 Cannes clerics
10 Sea-green
14 "___ said was ..."
15 Undergrowth
16 Legally invalid
17 Stallion shade
18 Deciduous tree
19 Hackman in *Runaway Jury*
20 Longest venomous snake
22 Pooch problem
23 It may be jotted
24 Argentine president (1974–76)
26 Keeps happening
29 Fondled
32 On the maternal side
33 Police shield
34 Mr. Iacocca
35 ___ *of the D'Urbervilles*
36 Sinks in the muck
37 Crichton's *Jurassic* ___
38 Sculptures and oils
39 Some sculptures
40 Fricke of country music
41 Giants
43 Collapsed in the clutch
44 Sister of Terpsichore
45 Sousaphone, for one
46 First month, alphabetically
48 History Channel reality show
53 Start up a computer
54 Stonehenge worshipper
55 Swedish furniture chain
56 Sites
57 Championship
58 Tiny bites
59 BPOE members
60 Dress down
61 Nephew of Cain

DOWN

1 Gospel author
2 Wellsian race
3 *The Good Earth* heroine
4 Hand-tighten fasteners
5 Monastery heads
6 Grease a palm
7 Raymond in *Rear Window*
8 Tomfoolery
9 "Mum's the word!"
10 Americans, south of the border
11 Brisbane locale
12 Forelimb bone
13 Pub brews
21 Reactor center
22 Out of the cage
25 10 million equal a joule
26 Put a new label on
27 Spanish year starter
28 *The Dead Zone* setting
29 Fruit vendors' stands
30 Creeptastic
31 Faked out, NHL-style
33 See
36 Jeff's tall pal
37 One of Rome's seven hills
39 Canaanite's deity
40 Monster.com listings
42 Optical inflammation
43 Supplied venture capital
45 Gabardine or serge e.g.
46 Up to snuff
47 Pocket billiards
49 Sonata, for one
50 Much in the same vein as
51 Auction vehicle, often
52 Fresh talk
54 Detox symptom

★ Word Sudoku

Complete the grid so that each row, each column and each 3 x 3 frame contains the nine letters from the black box below. The hidden nine-letter word is in the diagonal from top left to bottom right.

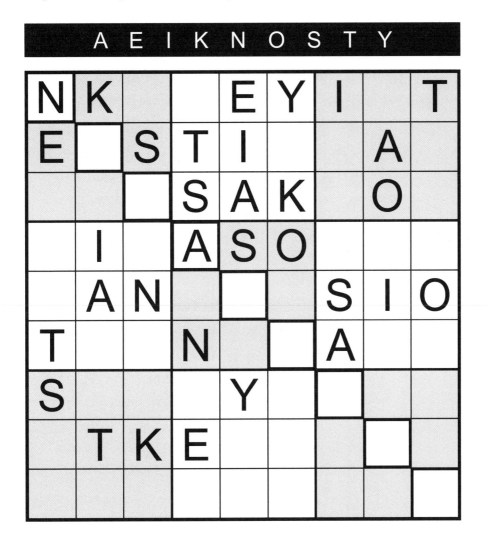

SANDWICH

What five-letter word belongs between the word at left and the word at right, so that the first and second word, and the second and third word, each form a common compound word or phrase?

GANG _ _ _ _ _ TON

★★ BrainSnack®—Missing Heart

Where (location 1–13) should the second 3 of hearts be placed?

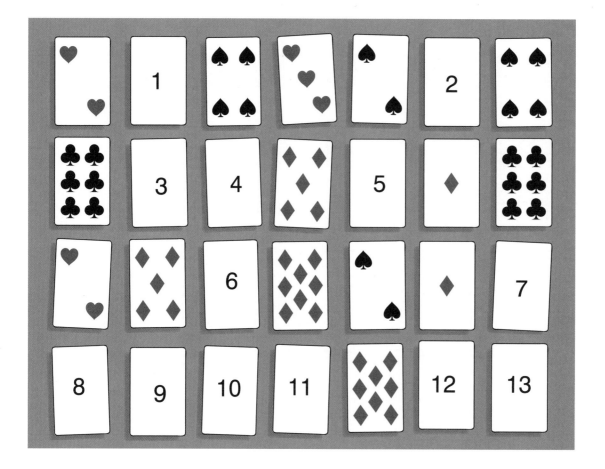

LETTERBLOCKS

Move the letterblocks around so that words are formed on top and below that you can associate with drinks.

★ The Midas Touch by Don Law

ACROSS

1 Grow friendly
5 Come in second at the track
10 Round top
14 *Class Reunion* novelist Jaffe
15 Sci-fi valet, maybe
16 Not have ___ to stand on
17 Prolific poet
18 Bathsheba's first mate
19 Young muchacho
20 Midas' favorite apple?
23 Rhodes locale
24 "Wonderful performance!"
25 Stewart or Steiger
26 Inhabit
31 Jacob wrestled one
34 Jai ___
35 "Golly!"
36 Midas' skydiving need?
40 ___ *tu* (Verdi aria)
41 Horned goddess
42 Detested
43 Adopted
46 Copy from a CD
47 Reindeer relative
48 Andes animal
52 Midas' dog?
58 Rapier relative
59 Where the eagle has landed
60 Little Dickens girl
61 What a stitch saves
62 Madea Simmons
63 Toledo's lake
64 Ravens or Orioles
65 Manicurist's board
66 Cannon in *Deathtrap*

DOWN

1 *Perry Mason* investigator
2 Gold medal, e.g.
3 Small lizard
4 Got off topic
5 Lopped off
6 ___ Voldemort
7 "___ Baby" (*Hair* song)
8 Furnace fuel
9 Lake Tana locale
10 Elton John song
11 Omnium-gatherum
12 Carte before the course
13 Star qualities?
21 Nice school?
22 Gulager in *McQ*
26 Mackinaw pattern
27 They're found in banks
28 Verge on
29 Bag with handles
30 Observed
31 *CIA Diary* author
32 Social standard
33 Silver-tongued
34 Altar locale
37 Sobriquet
38 Popular cook-off dish
39 Came to pass
44 Turn in for money
45 Ginger ___
46 Once in a blue moon
49 "And ___ fine fiddle had he ..."
50 Salsa legend Cruz
51 "Stormy Weather" composer
52 Bloke
53 Mayberry boy
54 Olin in *The Reader*
55 Paper measure
56 Kathryn of *Law & Order: CI*
57 Row or rank

★★ Binairo

Complete the grid with zeros and ones until there are 5 zeros and 6 ones in every row and every column. No more than two of the same number can be next to or under each other. Rows or columns with exactly the same content are not allowed. There is only one valid solution.

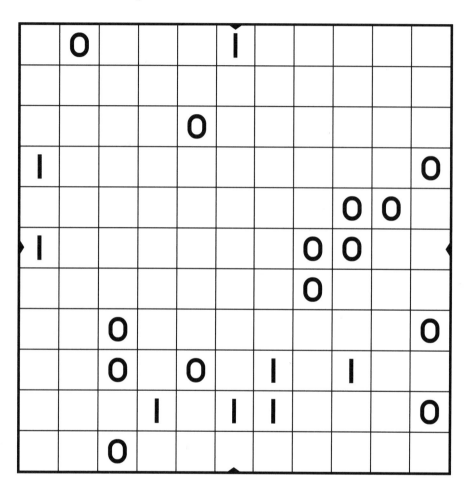

REPOSITION PREPOSITION

Unscramble ETCH TWO TRIPES and find a three-word preposition.

★ Spot the Differences

Find the nine differences in the image on the right.

DOUBLETALK

What word means "actions or reactions" or "to direct"?

★ Daddy Ditties by Peggy O'Shea

ACROSS

1 Camp David Accords nation
6 Campus marching group
10 Square column
14 Innes of *The Event*
15 Sushi fish
16 Goggle-eye fish
17 1983 Michael Keaton film
18 Bond girl Hatcher
19 "Ooh ___!"
20 1986 Madonna hit
23 Sunday in "There Will Be Blood"
24 Pal of Larry and Curly
25 Fettuccine ___
29 Yokel
33 Agile mountain animals
34 Clear wrongs
36 Japanese caldera
37 None at all
38 Track prey
39 Gives a color treatment to
40 And so forth
41 Friend of Gandhi
42 *The Wreck of the Mary ___* (1959)
43 Considering that
45 Flabbergasted
47 Overhead rails
48 Jungle cuckoo
49 1954 Perry Como hit
57 "Oh dear!"
58 Émile Zola classic
59 Ominous card
61 Hawaiian goose
62 Speller's clarifying phrase
63 Troop's camping place
64 "Faint heart ___ won ...": Cervantes
65 Mother of Pollux
66 Doltish

DOWN

1 Stately tree
2 *The World According to ___* (1982)
3 Native Arizonan
4 Investment choice
5 South-of-the-border fare
6 Prefix for tiller
7 Sign word
8 Like sourballs
9 Striped squirrel
10 Zonked out
11 SEC overseer
12 Shower powder
13 Stage actress Menken
21 Performed
22 Eternal City
25 Chloë of *Celtic Woman*
26 Detest
27 Absurdity
28 "Gadzooks!" et al.
29 Hard pill to swallow
30 Lake Placid craft
31 River in France
32 Just beat (with "out")
35 Swabbie
38 Like corn and apples
39 Ravage
41 *The Haunting* heroine
42 Gave blood
44 Tom Clancy fan
46 Cheese go-with
49 Ivy League team, commonly
50 Tommie of the '69 Amazin' Mets
51 Shower-door piece
52 Ming Dynasty collectible
53 Dame Lyons of Australia
54 Yemeni capital
55 High-fiber cereal
56 Cry over spilled milk
60 Souvenir shirt

★ Cage the Animals

Draw lines to completely divide up the grid into small squares with exactly one animal per square. The squares should not overlap.

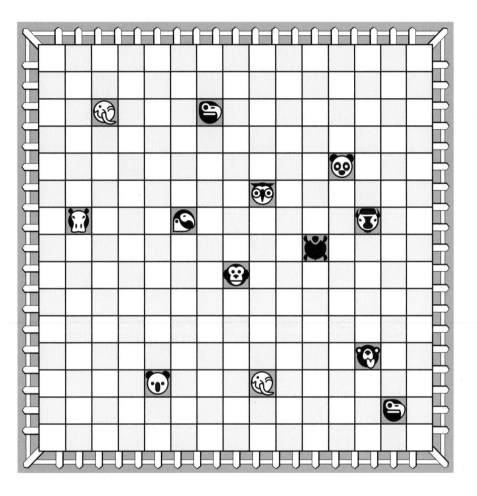

TRANSADDITION

Add one letter to ARISE and rearrange the rest to find a connection.

★ Antiquity

All the words are hidden vertically, horizontally or diagonally—in both directions. The letters that remain unused form a sentence from left to right.

```
B A B Y L O N E G A H T R A C
A N T I Q U I T I Y S G E N E
P H I L O S O P H Y R T A A L
L E Y R I E O F E C R S L F T
S O R B T I D I M A R Y P E H
E P U U H C N P E E R I H U C
O N O T T I I A D S T H A D A
A O E E E A S S I A T I B A B
E I G P H U R T S R N I E L N
T T N E E C T E O A E S T I S
P P W C M R I O T R L B T S L
Y I H T A O S I N I Y C I M A
G R E E C E R I H S L E I N V
E C E T R U S C A N N T I R E
H S O D A N T I Q U E H U C R
U N U M I S M A T I C S T I Y
N I O N O F P A P Y R U S W R
S I T E P I G R A P H Y I N G
```

CLASSIC
EGYPT
EPIGRAPHY
ETHIOPIA
ETRUSCAN
FEUDALISM
GREECE
HISTORY
HUNS
IBERIAN
INCA
INSCRIPTION
LITERATURE
MAURITANIA
NUMISMATICS
PAPYRUS
PERSIA
PHILOSOPHY
PYRAMID
ROME
SLAVERY
TEUTONS

ALPHABET	BABYLON	CELTS
ANTIQUE	CAESAR	CHEOPS
ANUBIS	CARTHAGE	CHINA

MISSING LETTER PROVERB

Fill in each missing letter, indicated by an X, to make a well-known proverb.

TXX MOXE TXX MEXXIEX

★★ Sunny Weather

Where will the sun shine? With the knowledge that each arrow points to a place where a symbol should be, can you locate the sunny spots? The symbols cannot be next to each other vertically, horizontally or diagonally. A symbol cannot be placed on top of an arrow. We show one symbol.

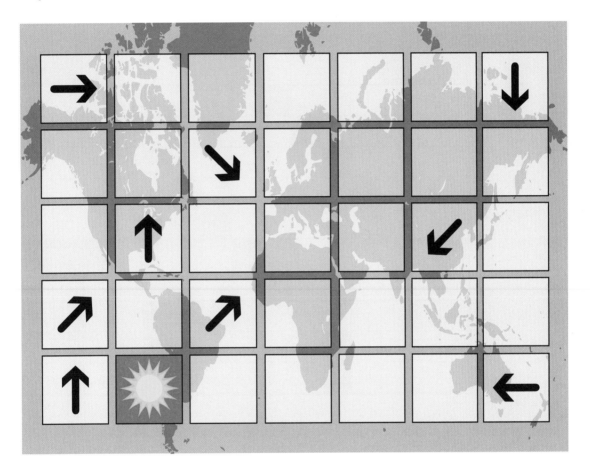

BLOCK ANAGRAM

Form the words that are described in the brackets with the letters above the grid. Extra letters are already in the right place.

GUILLOTINE (fee for education)

★ Themeless by Ralph Small

ACROSS

1 Figure heads?
5 Details, briefly
10 Fat farms
14 Dice spin
15 Like most Indians
16 Gardner or Kenton
17 Jai ___
18 Imprudent
20 Greek god of dreams
22 Chessmen
23 Lurid fiction
24 Auburn dye
25 Ride (on)
28 Clementine
31 Bridget Riley's genre
32 Cheeky
33 Prefix for bar
34 First-class
35 Tube-shaped pasta
36 Nap sacks
37 Netherlands city
38 Treasure container
39 Round bread loaf
40 Backside
42 Perceives
43 Gold-loving king
44 Hit a fly
45 Hand warmers
47 Lead and gold
51 His bullets are silver
53 Oliver Twist's entreaty
54 Writer of "Happy Birthday"
55 Israeli desert region
56 Preside at tea
57 Clothing-store section
58 Eat a bit
59 Monkey's home

DOWN

1 Bone up for an exam
2 Horseback sport
3 Controversial fruit spray
4 Indoor footwear
5 Police badge
6 Betty Grable was one
7 These may be tight or split
8 Forum 401
9 Hitchcock specialty
10 Williams of tennis
11 Hazardous
12 Downwind, at sea
13 Jazz groupings
19 "Get along home" girl of song
21 Pursue
24 Lacks, briefly
25 Coddled
26 Horatian poetry form
27 These bills are wanted?
28 Imposing residence
29 Pineapple fiber
30 Attendance count, perhaps
32 Clairvoyants
35 Long-tailed game bird
36 Intense disdain
38 Kind of vinegar
39 Two-by-four
41 Afton and Avon
42 Veer
44 A winter woe
45 Like sleazy salesmen
46 Crazy in la cabeza
47 Poacher's meal?
48 Wife of Hussein I
49 Faithful
50 Very dry
52 Teachers' union

★ Kakuro

Each number in a black area is the sum of the numbers that you have to enter in the next empty boxes. The empty boxes that make up the sum are called a run. The sum of the across run is written above the diagonal in the black area and the sum of the down run is written below the diagonal. Runs can only contain the numbers 1 through 9 and each number in a run can only be used once. The gray boxes only contain odd numbers and the white only even numbers.

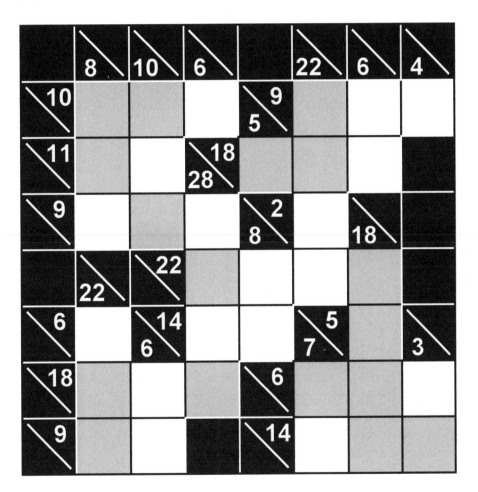

ONE LETTER LESS OR MORE

The word on the right side contains the letters of the word on the left side plus or minus the letter in the middle. One letter is already in the right place.

G E N E R O U S -E ☐ ☐ R ☐ ☐ ☐ ☐

★★★ BrainSnack®—Curl It

Where (1–14) will yellow team's fourth curling stone come to rest?

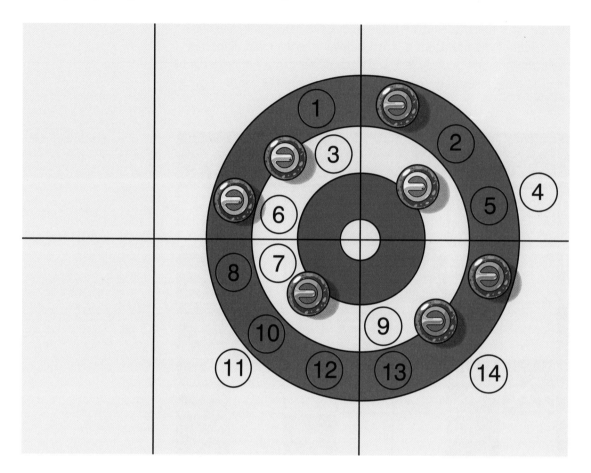

END GAME

The words you are seeking all have the letters END in them in the position indicated.
When you have found all of the answers, from the clues on the right, one column will reveal the
END GAME word which will give plenty of sheets.

E N D _ _ _ _ _	Surrounds a seed in a fruit
_ _ _ E N D _ _	Resisted an attack
E N D _ _ _ _ _	Intestinal worm
_ E N D _ _ _ _	French national policeman

★ Sky Sights by Peggy O'Shea

ACROSS

1 ASAP in the OR
5 Still-hunt
10 Munsters' pet dragon
14 Woody's heir
15 Final strike
16 "See ya," in Sorrento
17 Blind, in falconry
18 Wear the crown
19 Industrial region of Germany
20 George Harrison song
23 Sitting on top of
24 Detroit union
25 Fruity quaff
26 Pedicab kin
31 HP tablet
34 Miss an easy putt
35 Heady brew
36 Moniker
37 Counterfeit
38 Judge the merits of
39 Sunlamp ray
40 Gettysburg general
41 Fabulous Greek
42 Hippie headwear
44 Atlanta station
45 Moose cousin
46 Catholic clerics
50 Infrequently
55 Use a harvester
56 Religion of Pakistan
57 *Time* 2005 Person of the Year
58 Window frame
59 Cameron's *Shrek* role
60 Villain's look
61 One-time orchard spray
62 Consumed
63 Australian salt lake

DOWN

1 2011 First Family member
2 Joyce Kilmer poem
3 Open-eyed
4 Brook
5 Moved with authority
6 Topic
7 "Video" singer India.___
8 Piano supports
9 Home of Mammoth Cave
10 Threaded bolts
11 Name of 12 popes
12 Waikiki locale
13 In tatters
21 Derby winner Funny ___
22 Cod relative
26 Valerie Harper series
27 Skye in *River's Edge*
28 2011 FedEx Cup winner
29 Countertenor
30 "Read 'em and ___"
31 Purposely ignore
32 Mauna Loa scoria
33 To ___ (everyone)
34 Honolulu-based detective
37 Whittling tool
38 Appear like
40 French Sudan, today
41 Anne Nichols hero
43 Farther down
44 Fair Deal proponent
46 Make smooth
47 Hog caller's cry
48 Copier cartridge
49 Snooze loudly
50 Killer whale
51 Patricia in *Hud*
52 Javier's home
53 Global land mass
54 Record blemish

★★ Keep Going

Start on a blank square of your choice and connect as many blank squares as possible with one single continuous line. You can only connect squares along vertical and horizontal lines, not along diagonal lines. You must continue the connecting line up until the next obstacle, i.e., the rim of the box, a black square or a square that has already been used. You can change direction at any obstacle you meet. Each square can only be used once. The number of blank squares that will be left unused is marked in the upper square. There is more than one solution. We only show one solution.

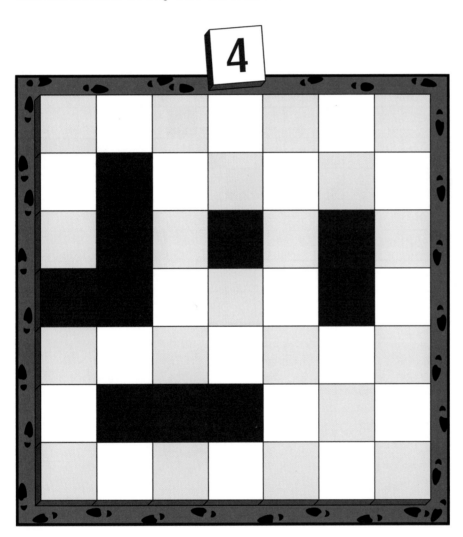

DELETE ONE

Delete one letter from BAIL IT and rearrange the rest to find a reason for release.

★★★ Sudoku

Fill in the grid so that each row, each column and each 3 x 3 frame contains every number from 1 to 9.

			2					
	7				4			
	8	2	3	7				
								5
	5		6		1			
3	6			8	5		1	
5	7		1	4	3			
	4	9		6		1		3
			8		7		4	

CHANGELINGS

Each of the three lines of letters below spell words which have an architechural connection, but the letters have been mixed up. Four letters from the first word are now in the third line, four letters from the third word are in the second line and four letters from the second word are in the first line. The remaining letters are in their original places. What are the words?

```
S O U N D A K R P N
Q U Y S C D A G E R
F T A I R A N O L E
```

★ Movies by Karen Peterson

ACROSS

1 South Sea isle
5 Big tooth
10 Cheerless
14 In the thick of
15 Weigh in
16 Blade
17 Singular
18 "Amazing" debunker
19 Snitched
20 2011 Woody Allen film
23 Refrain snippet
24 "___ need to explain?"
25 Tenor Pavarotti
29 Guys
33 Use the soapbox
34 Decathlete Thompson
36 Sheepish sound
37 SpongeBob's pet snail
38 Come again
39 Whip mark
40 Rescuer of Odysseus
41 Riga denizens
42 Comedienne Radner
43 Circle-drawing tool
45 Troublemaker
47 Commando weapon
48 Will Smith, to Willow
49 2011 Steve Carell film
58 City in Poland
59 Caesar's wear
60 Pop hero
61 Kapoor in *Slumdog Millionaire*
62 Make into law
63 Took a spill
64 Liver paste
65 Office staples
66 Life of Riley

DOWN

1 Lip protector
2 Mine, to Mimi
3 "Swedish Nightingale" Jenny
4 Kind of theft
5 Saddle horse
6 Bright aquarium fish
7 Dryer fluff
8 Don McLean's "___ Love You So"
9 Christmas lawn decoration
10 Item
11 Smell
12 Wrinkly tangelo
13 1981 Nicholson film
21 *Dies* ___ (Latin hymn)
22 Prefix for ester
25 Spock trademark
26 Heavenly prefix
27 Billiard shot
28 *Golden Boy* playwright
29 Five diamonds, to Annie Duke
30 Daggers in manuscripts
31 Mr. Magoo's nephew
32 Antichrist
35 Work on Broadway
38 Put up a fight
39 Safari subjects
41 Like malingerers
42 Ecstatic
44 Acrostic, for one
46 Commands
49 Give an ovation
50 *Five Women* author Jaffe
51 Mine access
52 Whistler's effort
53 Some, in Seville
54 Miner's tool
55 Concert halls
56 U. of Tennessee team
57 *Legally Blonde* heroine

★★★ Sport Maze

Draw the shortest way from the ball to the goal. You can only move along vertical and horizontal lines, not along diagonal lines. The figure on each square indicates the number of squares the ball must be moved in the same direction. You can change direction at each stop.

LETTER LINE

Put a letter in each of the squares below to make a word which means "a place of study." These numbered clues refer to other words which can be made from the whole.

4 3 6 9 1 5 7 EXAMPLES OF MORAL EXCELLENCE;
7 1 6 4 5 10 INSPECT; 4 5 3 2 7 TUBES;
9 1 2 5 6 7 DEVICES TO SELECT SIGNALS.

1	2	3	4	5	6	7	8	9	10

★ Word Sudoku

Complete the grid so that each row, each column and each 3 x 3 frame contains the nine letters from the black box below. The hidden nine-letter word is in the diagonal from top left to bottom right.

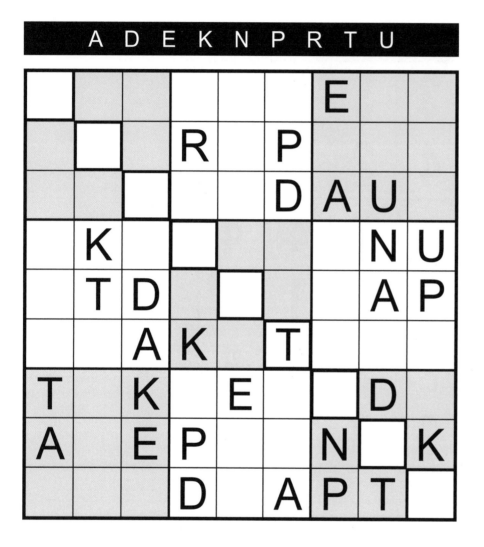

ONE LETTER LESS OR MORE

The word on the right side contains the letters of the word on the left side plus or minus the letter in the middle. One letter is already in the right place.

★★★ BrainSnack®—Fencing

Which post (1–4) should replace the arrow?

UNCANNY TURN

Rearrange the letters of the phrase to form a cognate anagram, one which is related or connected in meaning to the original phrase. The answer can be one or more words.

AN OLD SHOE

★ Temperature Extremes by John M. Samson

ACROSS

1 Present prettifiers
5 Conductor Sir Georg ___
10 Stereo's predecessor
14 Exercise aftermath
15 Beehive Stater
16 On ___ with (equal)
17 Stylish
18 Did some modeling
19 "Ooh ___!"
20 *M*A*S*H* nurse
23 Suffix for press
24 Oklahoma tribe
25 Web crawlers
29 Take a whack at
33 Diamond sides
34 ___ Haute, Indiana
36 Cars hit "You ___ the Girl"
37 Eagled a par-3 hole
38 "A ___ Day in London Town"
39 Lummox
40 Well-dressed fellow
41 Beatnik drum
42 To-do
43 Downright
45 Invalidate
47 Indian bean dish
48 Zippo
49 1995 Kate Beckinsale film
58 Kyrgyzstan border mountains
59 *The Great ___ Pepper* (1975)
60 Wished otherwise
61 Trig function
62 iPhone letters
63 Galena and limonite
64 Made a garden row
65 Ward off
66 Howling wind

DOWN

1 *Fiddle Fugue* composer
2 Eight, in Madrid
3 Iota
4 Out-of-the-way
5 Covered-dish ___
6 Great Plains Indians
7 Whip
8 Vincent van Gogh's brother
9 Diligence
10 Bad feeling
11 Moonfish
12 *The Lion King* character
13 Port in Algeria
21 Fits of rage
22 Tardy
25 Foul-up
26 Lace edging
27 Like Inspector Clouseau
28 Poker-faced
29 Vacuum tube filler
30 Aucklander, perhaps
31 Number on a liquor bottle
32 Soft fabric
35 *Back to the ___* (Wings album)
38 Not a leader
39 Jeremiah of song
41 Bric-a-___
42 Fly like a moth
44 Swirled
46 Open a sleeping bag
49 Mazuma
50 Potpourri
51 Memory ___
52 Auntie of Broadway
53 Brouhaha
54 *Garfield* dog
55 Mystique
56 Film spool
57 Goods: Abbr.

★ Cage the Animals

Draw lines to completely divide up the grid into small squares with exactly one animal per square. The squares should not overlap.

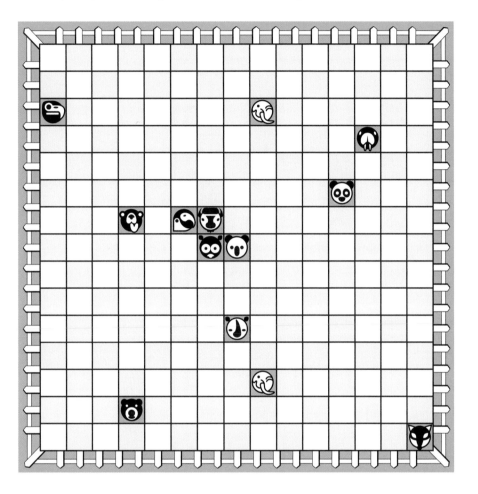

DOODLE PUZZLE

A doodle puzzle is a combination of images, letters and/or numbers that represent a word or a concept. If you cannot solve a doodle puzzle, do not look at the answer right away. Think hard—and outside the box.

★ Binairo

Complete the grid with zeros and ones until there are 6 zeros and 6 ones in every row and every column. No more than two of the same number can be next to or under each other. Rows or columns with exactly the same content are not allowed. There is only one valid solution.

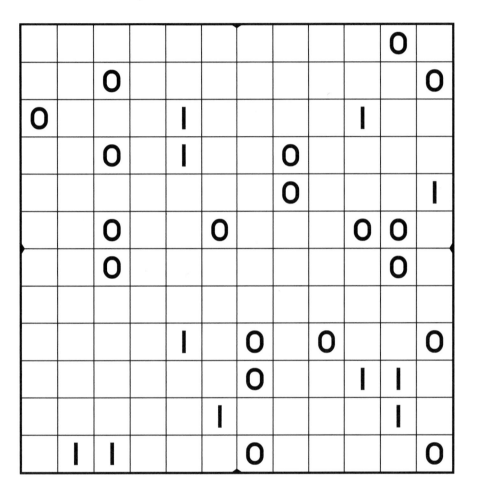

CHANGE ONE

Change one letter in each of these two words to form a common two-word phrase.

GULL GOWN

★★ On the Increase by John M. Samson

ACROSS

1 Extra dry
5 Lute of India
10 Con ___ (vigorously)
14 Moore in *Ghost*
15 Looking down
16 Canal section
17 Yemen neighbor
18 Make shadowy
19 Virginia willow
20 Song from *Jersey Boys*
23 Curved bench
24 ___-di-dah
25 Hops oven
27 Galena, for one
31 Catkin
34 Applications
36 Penlight battery
37 More important matters
41 Meadow
42 Sicilian volcano
43 Bar mitzvah et al.
44 Sneaky maneuvers
47 Shove off
49 Previous to
50 Puget Sound seaport
54 Reality show with weigh-ins
60 Magazine section
61 Glacial spur
62 "Ob-___, Ob-La-Da": Beatles
63 God of love
64 Hands (out)
65 S-shaped molding
66 Kal of *House*
67 *Cleopatra* setting
68 Not a hologram, say

DOWN

1 Acrobat maker
2 Modify a soundtrack
3 Spin doctor's product
4 Doorbell ring
5 Native Israelis
6 Genesis victim
7 Casting requirements?
8 Augustan Age poet
9 Total
10 Lighthearted
11 College drill team
12 Pastry specialist
13 "Fine by me"
21 Much more than miffed
22 Bert Bobbsey's twin
26 Decorative clusters
27 Rocky formations
28 Tom Sawyer's transport

29 Swiss river
30 Troubadour's tunes
31 Qualified
32 Conduct
33 Camelot oath
35 Impiety
38 Turncoat
39 *12 Angry Men* event
40 Mars black, e.g.
45 Like the phoenix
46 William Tell's home
48 Affirm to be true
51 Tributary of the Missouri
52 Jason's wife
53 *The Little Mermaid* character
54 Bend under a sink
55 Residence
56 Lord Wimsey's alma mater

57 Matey's libation
58 Hard to get hold of
59 Dance maneuver

★ BrainSnack®—Snow

Which group of snow crystals (2–5) is incorrect?

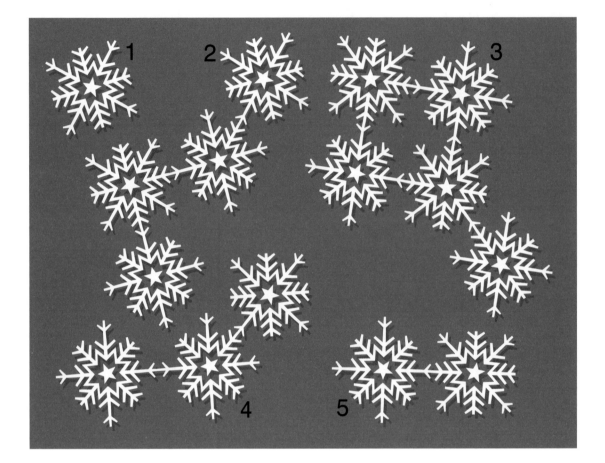

BLOCK ANAGRAM

Form the words that are described in the brackets with the letters above the grid. Extra letters are already in the right place.

MISCALLED (intermediate socioeconomic position)

			D							**S**

★ Space Travel

All the words are hidden vertically, horizontally or diagonally—in both directions. The letters that remain unused form a sentence from left to right.

```
I G R A V I T Y N A S W E R C
K C O D T H E S T A R D U S T
B E G I P C J M T C E J O R P
E L C R I C O U E N N I G N L
G O O F S S R L P P A C L E A
T B R V P N B H U I A V E E N
E L R H O B U S C M T S N I E
C N E A U Y A C H N B E N S T
N R T H B I A G E V U I R A O
E E D E S A A G U C C A A R I
I X E O R L I S E S M G L M D
C E P L I P S K U R A N U S B
S K Y L A B R U O G T I T T T
W A E O O A R I A N E S E R L
M O A P T S E R S R U O K O V
O E R A T A I K E E N R C N B
O Y T H E N U O N I T E O G D
N S T N E P T U N E A T R E S
```

ENTERPRISE
EXPLOSION
GAGARIN
GALILEO
GLENN
GRAVITY
HUBBLE
JUPITER
LAUNCH
MARS
MOON
NEPTUNE
PLANETOID
PROBE
PROJECT
ROCKET
SATURN
SCIENCE
SKYLAB
STARDUST
URANUS
VOYAGER

APOLLO	ATMOSPHERE	COLUMBIA
ARIANE	BAIKONUR	CREW
ARMSTRONG	CIRCLE	DOCK

FRIENDS

What do the following words have in common?

**YARD WRECK MATES LOAD
SHAPE OWNER WRIGHT**

★★ Pretty Beat-Up by Tim Wagner

ACROSS

1 Sackcloth material
5 Scruggs' bluegrass partner
10 Tag with a PG, e.g.
14 Eternally
15 Kind of show
16 Utilizer
17 Stand up
18 *Absolutely Fabulous* character
19 Visited
20 Maryland state flowers
23 Lemon of *30 Rock*
24 U.S. Open entrant
25 Italian toast
28 Uncredited credit, in quotes
30 Muppet eagle
33 It may be humble
34 Melville romance
35 Stadium audience participation
36 Elite study group
39 Exercise routine count
40 Baby bottle contents
41 Inventor Ampere
42 "___ he drove out of sight ..."
43 Mention in support, as a case
44 Enkindle
45 Portray
46 Teachers' org.
47 Pretty beat up
56 Biblical shipbuilder
57 Shire in *Rocky*
58 Tupper of Tupperware
59 Cube maker Rubik
60 Plain to see
61 Historians' study
62 Pal of wash
63 Dodger of Cooperstown
64 Garage event

DOWN

1 Coriander, e.g.
2 It isn't good
3 Badlands rise
4 Thwarts
5 Immobilize
6 Pink ___ cocktail
7 Indy speedster Luyendyk
8 See to
9 Measured dose
10 Rene in *Big Trouble*
11 Clueless
12 *High School Musical* extra
13 Diving eagles
21 Forged check passer
22 Capacious vase
25 British cavalry sword
26 More talented

27 Watchmaker's aid
28 Unhurried walk
29 Barnes & Noble tablet
30 Freeman or Patty
31 Duck
32 Saloon brawl
34 Death notice
35 Hopefuls
37 Rich Little, for one
38 Called by loudspeaker
43 A quarter of M
44 Inherent
45 Antonym for adore
47 From scratch
48 Collective wisdom
49 Turner in *Madame X*
50 Spelunking site
51 "Death and Fire" artist Paul
52 Don't put these on!

53 "Tomb Raider" heroine
54 River of Europe and Asia
55 The other thing

★★ Keep Going

Start on a blank square of your choice and connect as many blank squares as possible with one single continuous line. You can only connect squares along vertical and horizontal lines, not along diagonal lines. You must continue the connecting line up until the next obstacle, i.e., the rim of the box, a black square or a square that has already been used. You can change direction at any obstacle you meet. Each square can only be used once. The number of blank squares that will be left unused is marked in the upper square. There is more than one solution. We only show one solution.

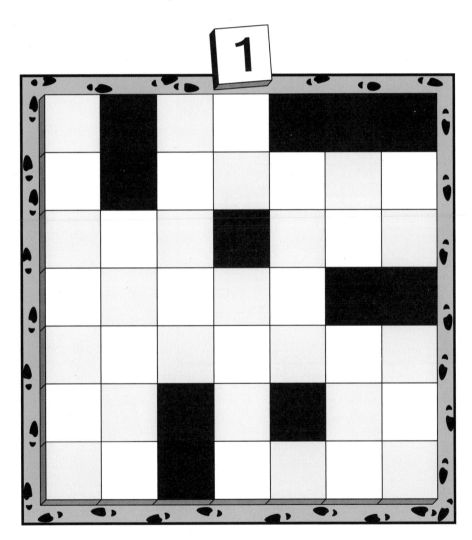

REPOSITION PREPOSITION

Unscramble A TIGHTER WORD and find a three-word preposition.

★★ Sudoku

Fill in the grid so that each row, each column and each 3 x 3 frame contains every number from 1 to 9.

5	7	4	6			1	9		
1			9	7					
2		8	5			6		7	
7			1	8		2	4		
	2	9							
8				9	4				
3	4						5		
	1		7				6		

SANDWICH

What four-letter word belongs between the word at left and the word at right, so that the first and second word, and the second and third word, each form a common compound word or phrase?

CROSS _ _ _ _ BREAK

★★ High by Karen Peterson

ACROSS

1 "Mayday!"
5 Mardi Gras necklaces
10 ___ and starts
14 Mishmash
15 Match up
16 Hydroxyl compound
17 World Cup cheers
18 Wander mentally
19 Jean in *The Da Vinci Code*
20 HIGH
22 Revolve around
23 Cecil Day Lewis, e.g.
24 Emmy winner in *Roots*
26 Lets
29 Foremost
32 *Merrie Melodies* stars
33 ___ operandi
34 "Just ___ suspected!"
35 Rob of *Parks and Recreation*
36 Highland fling?
37 "Guys only" party
38 African cobra
39 Took on cargo
40 *Ice Age* sabertooth
41 Swabby
43 Binge
44 Party hearty
45 Flying prefix
46 Kind of role
48 HIGH
53 Hamlet's sister in comics
54 Sky, perhaps
55 Keep from escaping
56 Clive in *Duplicity*
57 Ryan in *Love Story*
58 Relaxation
59 Like valuable stamps
60 Tubular pasta
61 Nerve network

DOWN

1 Mr. Ed's foot
2 She outwrestled Thor
3 Willing, in verse
4 Table
5 Boy Scouts earn them
6 Crane kin
7 Domingo solo
8 Swindled
9 Ready to go
10 José in *The Caine Mutiny*
11 HIGH
12 Rafa Nadal's uncle
13 Where the coin goes
21 "___ that again?"
22 Addition column
25 Instigate
26 African mountains
27 At large
28 HIGH
29 Not plowed
30 Kansas river
31 Strictness
33 Stowe or Albright
36 Be solicitous
37 Nefarious
39 Take a bath
40 Laura in *Rambling Rose*
42 Manx, for one
43 Volkswagen
45 Beelike
46 2011 superhero film
47 Spirit Lake locale
49 Wolverine's group
50 *Dies* ___ (requiem hymn)
51 Huge
52 Olympic sword
54 Cut off

★ Word Sudoku

Complete the grid so that each row, each column and each 3 x 3 frame contains the nine letters from the black box below. The hidden nine-letter word is in the diagonal from top left to bottom right.

A	D	E	M	N	P	R	T	U

				M			R	
		A				M	N	U
			D					
N	T		E		U			
R		M	T					A
M		N	A	D	E			
D	R	U				A		N
E					N		M	D

LETTERBLOCKS

Move the letterblocks around so that words are formed on top and below that you can associate with bones.

★★★ Sport Maze

Draw the shortest way from the ball to the goal. You can only move along vertical and horizontal lines, not along diagonal lines. The figure on each square indicates the number of squares the ball must be moved in the same direction. You can change direction at each stop.

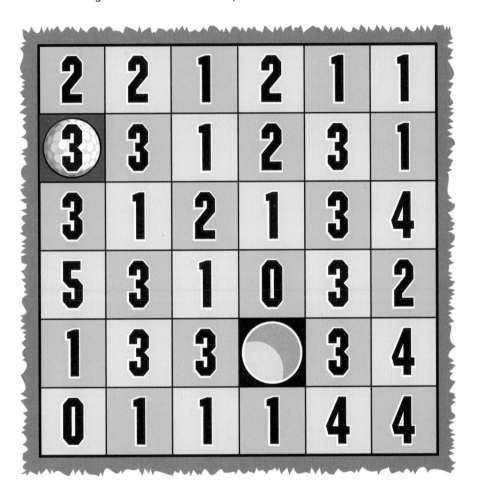

DOUBLETALK

What word means "to endorse" or "a punitive action"?

★★ Low by Karen Peterson

ACROSS

1 Bric-a-___
5 Typeface embellishment
10 Most Monets
14 Gray wolf
15 Feminist Jong
16 ___-jerk response
17 Straw in the wind
18 Grand
19 Whoop-de-do
20 LOW
22 One-legged skipper
23 Popeye, to Bluto
24 *The Last Days of Pompeii* heroine
26 Expunge
29 Newfoundland and ___
33 Looseness
34 Bear's disappointment
35 Andalusian article
36 Big top
37 Mountain feature
38 Roman 2,200
39 Suffix for humor
40 Jason's sorceress wife
41 Leaf found in Toronto
42 Taken for granted
44 Stopped, briefly
45 What yardbirds do
46 Make some money
47 Bloke
49 LOW
55 Yale team
56 Apollo's blood
57 Rested
58 Flat fee
59 Become weatherworn
60 Scandinavian royal
61 Lyra's brightest star
62 Taken for a ride
63 Diaphanous

DOWN

1 Special-interest group
2 Plum tomato
3 Harbor a fugitive, e.g.
4 Written agreement
5 Hard to rattle
6 Stiff-backed
7 Major Baltic port
8 Suffix for angel
9 Not perfect
10 Gold medalist Baiul
11 LOW
12 Luke Skywalker's sister
13 Novak Djokovic, for one
21 Roll of the dice
25 "Kid" of jazz
26 Prohibit legally
27 ___-de-lis
28 LOW

29 Loaded cargo
30 Aquarium growth
31 Male relative of Pierre
32 Competed at Indy
34 Midway attraction
37 Corrected
38 World's largest volcano
40 Uncommunicative
41 Anthony in *El Cantante*
43 Nicaraguan snooze
44 Matched up
46 Lyrical verse
47 *Jeopardy* creator Griffin
48 Protected, in boating
50 Tan
51 Place of business
52 South Pacific isle

53 Storyteller
54 Long to change places with

★★★ BrainSnack®—Honey Cell

Which cell (1–31) should be filled with honey?

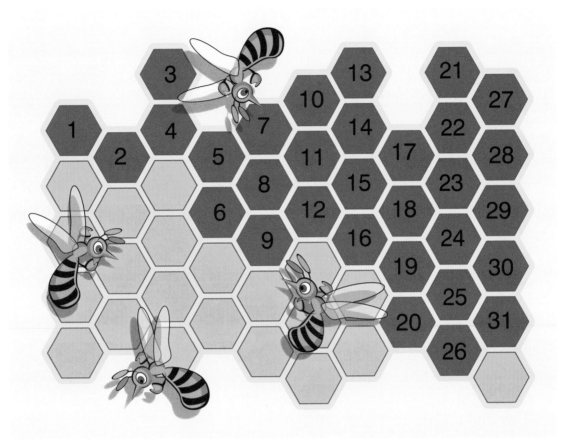

TRANSADDITION

Add one letter to TRAFFIC RULE and rearrange the rest to find a connection.

★ Sudoku Twin

Fill in the grid so that each row, each column and each 3 x 3 frame contains every number from 1 to 9. A sudoku twin is two connected 9 x 9 sudokus.

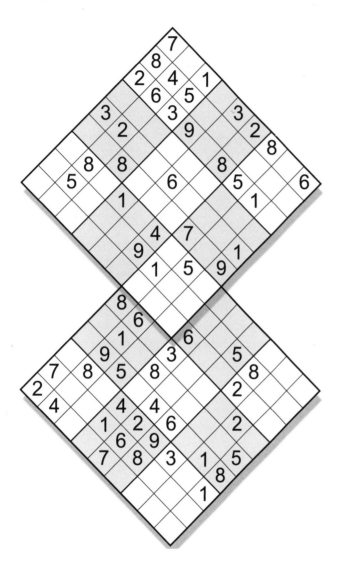

BLOCK ANAGRAM

Form the words that are described in the brackets with the letters above the grid. Extra letters are already in the right place.

SACRIFICIAL (unstable monetary situation)

★★ How Lovely! by Michele Sayer

ACROSS

1 Petri dish gelatin
5 Blocked from sunlight
10 Ebb antonym
14 Narrative
15 Conical domicile
16 Mote
17 Heron relative
18 "You ___ kidding!"
19 Apt anagram of "vile"
20 Amorous parrot
22 Walking leaf, e.g.
24 Aftershock
25 ___ standstill
26 Groundwork
29 Soda shop order
32 Golfer's dozen
35 Sidewalk marker
37 Pakistani airlines
38 Clarinet's kin
39 Simmons competitor
40 Talk like a toper
41 Escape or Explorer
42 Mrs. Nicolas Sarkozy
43 Fine-grained silt
44 Surround-sound device
46 Pale purple
48 Bats
49 Ducked
53 Auto IDs
56 Romantic goings-on
58 "I swear" may start it
59 Papas or Dunne
61 Golf club feature
62 Fewer than twice
63 The Archfiend
64 Britt of *Desperate Housewives*
65 *The Wizard of Oz* star
66 Cleans up copy
67 Fast bucks?

DOWN

1 Out of whack
2 Eva of *Green Acres*
3 Having a pulse
4 Look like
5 Way up
6 Cologne chap
7 Wasn't original
8 Lounge locale
9 Himalayan hulk
10 Pamplona party
11 Tomato
12 Of the ear
13 Kelly or Disney
21 Pythons
23 DEA agent
27 Cupcake coverer
28 ___ *We Dance* (2004)
29 Emulate Superman
30 Common papal name
31 Teacup handles
32 Head honcho
33 Go right next to
34 No marriage of convenience
36 Jai ___
39 ___ Paulo, Brazil
40 Self-styled
42 End a chess game
43 Wash against
45 Somewhat
47 Carpentry tools
50 Semiconductor device
51 White in *Dreamgirls*
52 Dishearten
53 Shooting match?
54 Lang of Smallville
55 Distaff ___
56 A tribe of Israel
57 "Don't bet ___!"
60 VIP carpet color

★★ Sunny Weather

Where will the sun shine? With the knowledge that each arrow points to a place where a symbol should be, can you locate the sunny spots? The symbols cannot be next to each other vertically, horizontally or diagonally. A symbol cannot be placed on top of an arrow. We show one symbol.

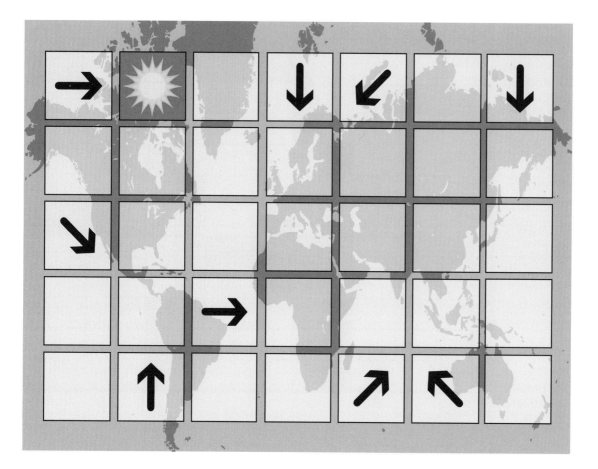

BLOCK ANAGRAM

Form the word that is described in the brackets with the letters above the grid. Extra letters are already in the right place.

HERNIA (cyclone)

★ Word Pyramid

Each word in the pyramid has the letters of the word above it, plus a new letter.

C

(1) Electric current
(2) Curve
(3) Black-and-white whale
(4) Nocturnal insect
(5) Performed by a choir
(6) Intestinal infection caused by ingestion
(7) Academic degree

MISSING LETTER PROVERB

Fill in each missing letter, indicated by an X, to make a well-known proverb.

XLX XOOX XXINXS MXST XOME XO AX XND

★ Safe Code

To open the safe you have to replace the question marks with the correct figures. You can find these figures by determining the logical methods behind the numbers shown. These methods may include calculation, inversion, repetition, chronological succession, forming ascending and descending series.

SAFE A08

END GAME

The words you are seeking all have the letters END in them in the position indicated. When you have found all of the answers, from the clues on the right, one column will reveal the END GAME word that your uncle will know well.

			E	N	D			Useful chart
_	E	N	D	_	_	_	_	A swinging weight
_	_	E	N	D	_	_	_	Paying out
_	E	N	D	_	_	_	_	A blood feud

★★ Literary Legends by Ralph Small

ACROSS

1 Help, as a lawbreaker
5 Alpine crest
10 Yearn
14 Teri in *Witches' Brew*
15 Morning's awakening
16 Bitty amount
17 *For Whom the Bell Tolls* author
20 Converse product
21 Hold contents
22 Sea salt?
23 Eggs
24 *The House at Pooh Corner* author
28 X-ray machines, e.g.
32 Sun-___ tomatoes
33 Digs for ore
35 Vacant space
36 You can see right through it
37 "Ten ___ a Dance"
38 Room at the Alhambra
39 Rescuer of Odysseus
40 Like some hosiery
41 Felicitously
42 Block
44 Tyrannize
46 "___ Fine Day": Chiffons
47 ___ tu (*A Masked Ball* aria)
48 Idolize
52 Facelift focus
56 *The Sound and the Fury* author
58 *A Little Night Music* heroine
59 Marathon hurdles
60 Neeson of *Rob Roy*
61 Wine price factor
62 Washington, but not Lincoln
63 Alcohol lamp

DOWN

1 A month of Sundays
2 Country ballroom?
3 European eagle
4 Agreements between nations
5 Behind, nautically
6 Essen river
7 Wind direction
8 Heartburn relief
9 Classic examples
10 Move to and fro
11 It's south of Minnesota
12 Bachelor party attendee
13 2010 WBA heavyweight champ
18 Medieval poet
19 Stellar explosions
24 Make it up as you go along
25 Boxing setting
26 Child
27 Big man in Oman
28 Start
29 Gladden hugely
30 Hamburger holders
31 Doesn't fold
34 Suffix for serpent
37 They're spotted in Africa
38 Light rain
40 Decalogue mount
41 Arbor Day month
43 Ocean wave
45 Go through
48 Chicago's "Look ___"
49 Sup in style
50 Humerus neighbor
51 Send out matter
52 Animation pioneer Disney
53 Do needle work.
54 Like Sprat's cuisine
55 Humorist Bombeck
57 Key West locale: Abbr.

★ Hourglass

Starting in the middle, each word in the top half has the letters of the word below it, plus a new letter, and each word in the bottom half has the letters of the word above it, plus a new letter.

(1) small computers with rotatable touchscreen
(2) conflict
(3) a piece of furniture
(4) second in order
(5) unclothed
(6) pause
(7) bread makers
(8) moneymen

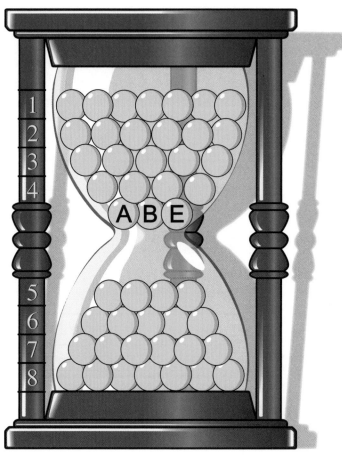

LETTER LINE

Put a letter in each of the squares below to make a word which means "a form of air transport." These numbered clues refer to other words which can be made from the whole.

1 6 8 9 3 LODGING;
7 4 3 6 8 DRIVER; 2 3 4 8 9 SUPERIOR;
7 10 4 5 2 COST.

1	2	3	4	5	6	7	8	9	10

★★ Keep Going

Start on a blank square of your choice and connect as many blank squares as possible with one single continuous line. You can only connect squares along vertical and horizontal lines, not along diagonal lines. You must continue the connecting line up until the next obstacle, i.e., the rim of the box, a black square or a square that has already been used. You can change direction at any obstacle you meet. Each square can only be used once. The number of blank squares that will be left unused is marked in the upper square. There is more than one solution. We only show one solution.

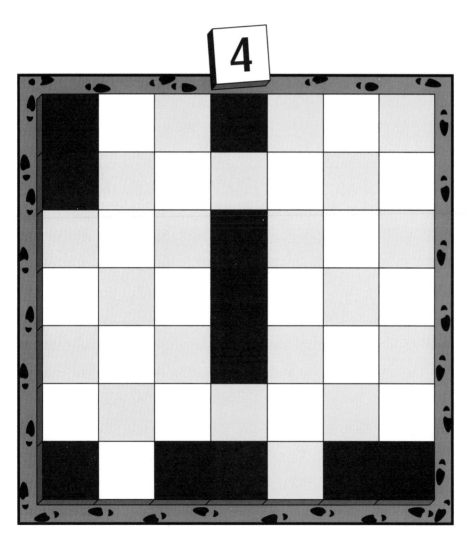

DELETE ONE

Delete one letter from I TEACH IRON JURORS and rearrange the rest to find young musicians.

★★ Twin Openers I by Michele Sayer

ACROSS

1 Burger side
5 Binary star in Perseus
10 Read optically
14 Bose system
15 Dutch cheese
16 Toontown murder victim
17 Turkey's neighbor
18 Like Gandhi
19 Husband of Osiris
20 Termite eater
22 Leaves on the table?
24 Enlightened
25 Chocolate sub
26 Self-proclaimed genius
29 TV adjustment
32 Conductor Previn
33 One of the Corleones
34 Common article
35 ___ to Perdition (2002)
36 Oceanic ray
37 Burn on the outside
38 Sleet-covered
39 Sharply felt
40 Mattress features
41 Chinese metropolis
43 Setting
44 Scale deductions
45 Sow's squeal
46 Goods cast overboard
48 It sticks to your ribs?
52 Salt Lake City locale
53 "Farewell, Pierre!"
55 2010 Disney sci-fi film
56 Carp kin
57 Tibia neighbors
58 Edvard Munch Museum site
59 Forest ruminants
60 Further
61 Dobbin's dinner

DOWN

1 LaBeouf of *Transformers*
2 Turkish currency
3 Long way off
4 Not on the lee side
5 Dumbstruck
6 Nantes river
7 Icky stuff
8 Idiosyncratic
9 Lake Geneva city
10 Shanty singer
11 2011 Yankee pitcher
12 Betwixt
13 Monstrous Scottish loch
21 Ivy feature
23 Affectedly aesthetic
25 Imaginative tale
26 Stade Roland Garros site
27 Arden of fiction
28 Historic 1944 event
29 Raccoonlike animal
30 Verb of the future
31 Succinct
33 Large seabirds
36 Diagrams
37 Parakeet's cousin
39 Pearl Mosque site
40 Negative aspects
42 Ramblers of yore
43 Part of LCD
45 Like Henry VIII
46 Law in *The Aviator*
47 List abbr.
48 Kookaburra, e.g.
49 ___ Minor
50 Filly's brother
51 Eve's grandson
54 Will Smith, to Willow

★★★ BrainSnack®—Cookies

Which icing cookie (1–5) should replace the question mark?

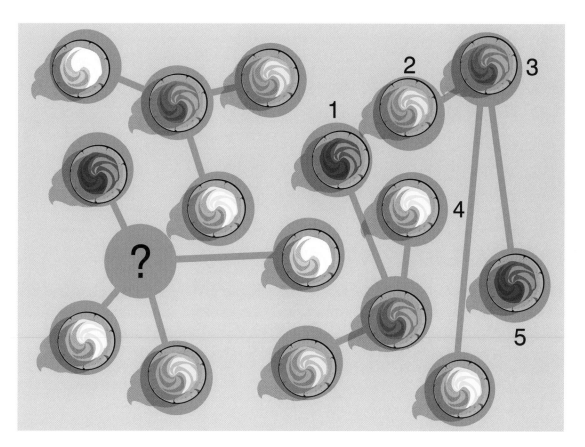

SQUIRCLES

Place consonants in the squares and vowels in the circles and form words in each vertical column. The definitions of the words you are looking for are listed. (The grid will reveal two musical instruments)

(1) Hit
(2) Have humps
(3) Once a year
(4) Promotional device
(5) Treat in a jar
(6) Not from this Earth
(7) Holder of paper
(8) Desirable bars

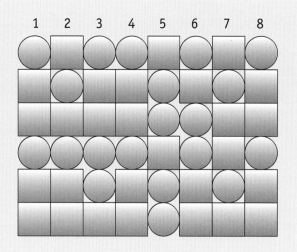

★ Actresses

All the words are hidden vertically, horizontally or diagonally—in both directions. The letters that remain unused form a sentence from left to right.

```
O A N A C D Z T H E P B U R N
B R E S S S N P E F R W O G T
R F O R I M H A E S O B I R O
A N A E T U H I L R E N N E D
G E W A P E F K R R T A O B R
R H I P O F E A T C A M T D A
A T E R E C F S A D L G S L B
F R N R A E P E A I E R I O R
T O Q P F O R R R E V E N G M
M W S U A N T T C T U B A E O
R Y C T E C N O S R E D N A T
I A H N E T A F W I N S L E T
I H N L W R T T L C E M E O E
F N E A T E U E L H D H S V C
O O I R M R A A O S A A O C W
N A D R N D T V R Y O O L N A
D C E E H A I W E L C H C R F
A A R C T E R K N R O L Y A T
```

DENEUVE
DIETRICH
ELECTRA
FARROW
FAWCETT
FONDA
FOSTER
GARBO
GARLAND
GOLDBERG
HAYEK
HAYWORTH
HEPBURN
HUPPERT
KIDMAN
LOREN
MONROE
PFEIFFER
ROBERTS
SCHNEIDER
SPACEK
STREEP
TAYLOR
TURNER
WEAVER
WEISZ
WELCH
WINSLET

ANDERSON   ARQUETTE   BERGMAN
ANISTON   BARDOT   CLOSE

ONE LETTER LESS OR MORE

The word on the right side contains the letters of the word on the left side plus or minus the letter in the middle. One letter is already in the right place.

B A C K D O O R +L ☐ ☐ **A** ☐ ☐ ☐ ☐ ☐

★★ Twin Openers II by Michele Sayer

ACROSS

1 Code word for "A"
5 Location
10 Puts in stitches
14 Antony or Chagall
15 Bar twist
16 Pressure from the cops
17 Nonesuch
18 ___-garde
19 Light brown shade
20 Founding member of Judas Priest
22 Mouse's find
23 Apiphobe's fear
24 Violinist Zimbalist
26 On ship
29 Indy racer Luyendyk
30 AWOL arresters
33 Cite verbatim
34 Sherlock's love
35 Gershwin or Newborn
36 Heidi's home
37 Did some karate
38 Cross condition
39 Air-gun ammo
40 Of birth
41 Greek S
42 Remote battery
43 Foamy drinks
44 Dark blue plum
45 Whirlpool appliance
47 Highway exit
48 Santa ___
50 *How Green Was My Valley* novelist
55 Exodus plague
56 *Fantastic Mr. Fox* author Dahl
57 Lionel Richie song
58 Alternative word
59 Month for fools
60 "Peter Pan" pirate
61 Tampa Bay team
62 "___ Train": Cat Stevens
63 Certain raspberry pastry

DOWN

1 Frenzied
2 Gangly
3 Allen of radio days
4 Circus stars
5 Smoothed wood
6 Jeans
7 "Walk Like ___": The Four Seasons
8 Snaky fish
9 Tolkien's Treebeard
10 Khan in *The Jungle Book*
11 *Tulips & Chimneys* author
12 Toasty
13 Paycheck leftover
21 "You ___ Meant for Me"
22 Ontario native
25 Pinpoint
26 Jordan seaport
27 *Taras ___*: Gogol
28 "Clumsy me!"
29 Zones
31 First-class
32 The Archfiend
34 Butt in
37 Curly-leaf cabbage
38 Most elementary
40 Opposing votes
41 Equivalent
44 Loiter
46 Parameters
47 Museum piece
48 Loire tributary
49 "Deck the Halls" syllables
51 Yuri Zhivago's love
52 Tibetan monk
53 Flanders river
54 Russian negative
56 Grammy category

★★ Number Cluster

Complete the grid by constituting adjoining clusters that consist of as many cubes as the number on the cubes. At cube 5, for instance, you will have to make a five-cube cluster. Two or more figure cubes of the same value belong to the same cluster. You can only place your cubes along horizontal and/or vertical lines.

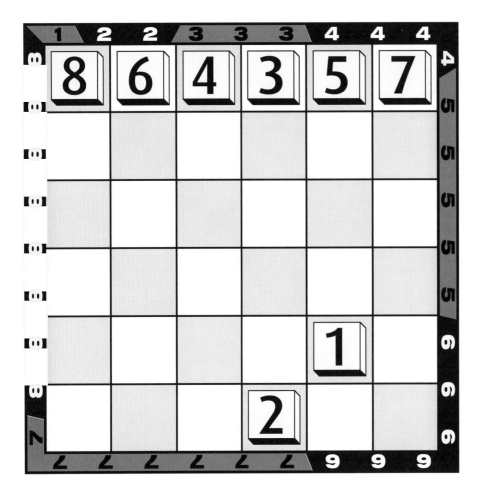

UNCANNY TURN

Rearrange the letters of the phrase to form a cognate anagram, one which is related or connected in meaning to the original phrase. The answer can be one or more words.

WORTH TEA

★★ BrainSnack®—Red Red Wine

Which Château Snack wine label (1–6) is fake?

DOODLE PUZZLE

A doodle puzzle is a combination of images, letters and/or numbers that represent a word or a concept. If you cannot solve a doodle puzzle, do not look at the answer right away. Think hard—and outside the box.

★★ Punny and Funny I by Tim Wagner

ACROSS

1 Ho-hum
5 Golden Globes genre
10 "Hurting ___ Other": Carpenters
14 It conquers all
15 Try to disprove
16 Turkish biggie
17 Split into pieces
18 Make law
19 "___and bear it"
20 How to race in the Rolex 24 at Daytona?
23 Tack item
24 Slap-happy stooge
25 ___ old how
26 Down payments
31 Driving problem
34 Country singer Travis
35 One who handles bookings?
36 ___-poly
37 Lines on leaves
38 Norm's wife on *Cheers*
39 Not lately
40 Garçon's counterpart
41 Halloween beverage
42 Like a roc
44 Bamboozles
45 Granola piece
46 Bulletins
50 Tennis ace?
55 It hangs out on the roof
56 Movie sections
57 Passions, to Pliny
58 Epiphanic cries
59 In a snit
60 Naldi of silent movies
61 Litter littlest
62 Play dough
63 Saintly

DOWN

1 Thespian Bernhardt
2 Alpha's opposite
3 Fishing boat device
4 Commonplace
5 White-tie
6 Gets a flat
7 Blind as ___
8 Considerably
9 Goes for
10 "Take It Easy" group
11 Soil: Comb. form
12 Trendy
13 Williams Jr. of Nashville
21 Honolulu Zoo bird
22 Rail family bird
26 Bore
27 Berlin article
28 Coated cupcakes

29 Rushed
30 Pull one's punches
31 Apothecary measure
32 Far from peppy
33 Zillions
34 Honduras port
37 Ford Crown ___
38 Calling on
40 Ferrari parent
41 Blanchett in *The Aviator*
43 "I kid you not"
44 Engine power, informally
46 Nick in *Hotel Rwanda*
47 Objet d'art
48 Poetic muse
49 Links legend Sam
50 Bottom-heavy fruit
51 Island near Kauai

52 Terrible czar
53 Lobby plant
54 Trig

★★★ Sport Maze

Draw the shortest way from the ball to the goal. You can only move along vertical and horizontal lines, not along diagonal lines. The figure on each square indicates the number of squares the ball must be moved in the same direction. You can change direction at each stop.

CHANGE ONE

Change one letter in each of these two words to form a common two-word phrase.

CAKE RACK

★ Word Sudoku

Complete the grid so that each row, each column and each 3 x 3 frame contains the nine letters from the black box below. The hidden nine-letter word is in the diagonal from top left to bottom right.

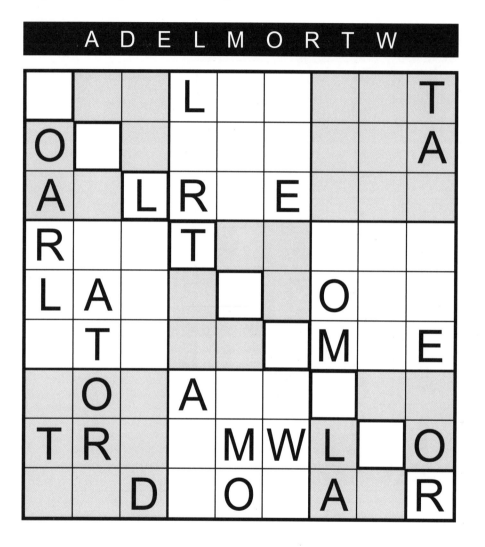

LETTERBLOCKS

Move the letterblocks around so that words are formed on top and below that you can associate with trees.

★★ Themeless by Ralph Small

ACROSS

1 Snorkasaurus of Bedrock
5 Kind of boom
10 Autobiographer's subject
14 Month before Nisan
15 Dispatch craft
16 Word after pig or pony
17 Breakfast cereal
19 Pigmentary eye layer
20 Grow more intense
21 Hardly grand
23 Glutton's cry
24 Leary in *The Ref*
25 Like wasp nests
28 Ski lodge drink
31 Beard of the WNBA
32 Backyard courtyard
33 Fish eggs
34 Small pastry
35 Instrument of old
36 Anagram name of Nora
37 Refrain syllable
38 Stale and then some
39 John Paul I and II
40 Not expressly stated
42 Jacqueline in *Bullitt*
43 Ancient serf
44 "Clair de ___": Debussy
45 Chosen pursuit
47 What odometers measure
51 Get wind of
52 Gossamer
54 Scots tongue
55 Manny's *Ice Age* love
56 Rule of thumb
57 Three-___ woodpecker
58 Monopoly pile
59 Kathryn of *Law & Order: CI*

DOWN

1 Carp kin
2 Rite answers
3 Undercover buster
4 Tannenbaum trinket
5 Worker's compensation
6 Football-shaped
7 Goddess of victory
8 Expert finish
9 Avon offering
10 Small apartment
11 Listens secretly
12 Polygraph spikes
13 Black key, maybe
18 Regional foliage
22 "Hang ___ your hats!"
24 Fussed over
25 Actress LuPone
26 Burglar ___
27 Put another way

28 It's done again and again
29 Recipient of gifts
30 Baking necessity
32 One sort of larceny
35 Taped
36 Comedienne Barr
38 Dossier
39 Carvel of 1492
41 Eyed rudely
42 Scrubs
44 Fatty acid, e.g.
45 Atkins of Nashville
46 Prefix for space
47 Racer Earnhardt
48 Former Jordanian queen
49 Scale back
50 Carlisle Cullen's wife
53 O'Neill sea play

★★★ Sudoku

Fill in the grid so that each row, each column and each 3 x 3 frame contains every number from 1 to 9.

				3				
			2		8			
	7		9			4		
	6						5	7
		3				9	4	6
9	4			6	1		8	
				2		5		8
6	3			7	4			9
2							6	4

FRIENDS

What do the following words have in common?

CONTENT FORMATION FUNCTION TREATMENT ADMINISTRATION

★★★ BrainSnack®—Olives

Which group of three olives should replace the question mark above the lettered olives? Answer like this: BDD.

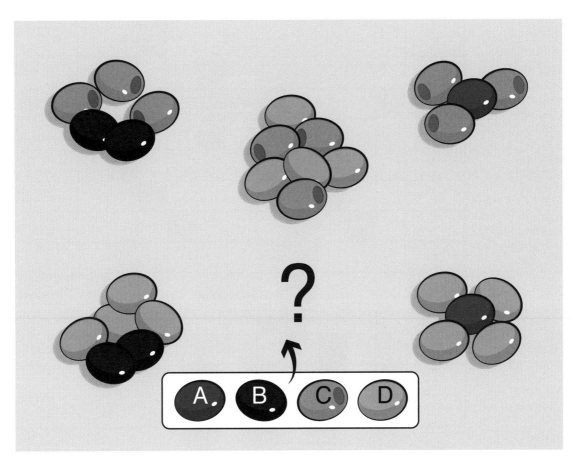

SANDWICH

What five-letter word belongs between the word at left and the word at right, so that the first and second word, and the second and third word, each form a common compound word or phrase?

E L K _ _ _ _ _ D O G

★★★ Title Roles by John M. Samson

ACROSS

1 Security problem
5 2004 Jude Law role
10 Like trade-ins
14 Ford model
15 "Oh boy!"
16 Redneck's red area
17 Beau Geste in *Beau Geste* (1939)
19 Marine heading
20 Demolition derby aftermath
21 Symbol
23 Make a doily
24 Callaway of golf
25 More than half
30 Doobie
33 Starchy collars
34 "Strike up the band!"
36 Composer Newborn
37 1972 U.S. Open finalist
38 Managed
39 Bench
40 X, at times
41 Sophia in *Two Women*
42 Living proof?
43 Like shuffleboard boards
45 Left on base
47 Yang's companion
48 Like 1 or 3
49 Used what was available
52 Resting places
57 Bellicose god
58 Hud in *Hud* (1963)
60 Ready for plucking
61 Perennial herb
62 Film composer Rota
63 Jabbers
64 Former teen magazine
65 Ragout

DOWN

1 Gangster Diamond
2 Round cheese
3 City near New Delhi
4 ___ Kops
5 Mexican rodent
6 Chicago district
7 Fancy Dans
8 Suffix for cyan
9 Thornfield Hall governess
10 Helpless
11 Norma Rae in *Norma Rae* (1979)
12 Electric sword
13 Judge to be
18 Converts to carbon
22 Say hello to
25 Deli display
26 Confused
27 Ed Wood in *Ed Wood* (1994)
28 God of thunder
29 "Holy cow!"
30 Weed out
31 Hit the backspace key
32 Ranked
35 Camper's shelter
38 Food fish
39 Oft-photographed times
41 Do a bank job
42 Mission priest
44 Printing daggers
46 *The Wizard of Id* knight
49 Grand old name
50 Song from *La Tosca*
51 Goes for
52 Bargains
53 Titular O'Neill trees
54 Pass by
55 Buffalo feature
56 Mauna Kea's cap
59 "Eureka!"

★ Spot the Differences

Find the nine differences in the image on the right.

LETTERBLOCKS

Move the letterblocks around so that words are formed on top and below that you can associate with Christmas characters.

★ Horoscope

Fill in the grid so that every row, every column and every frame of six boxes contains six different symbols: health, work, money, happiness, family and love. Look at the row or column that corresponds with your sign of the zodiac and find out which symbols are important for you today. The symbols appear in increasing order of importance (1–6). It's up to you to interpret the meaning of each symbol to your specific situation.

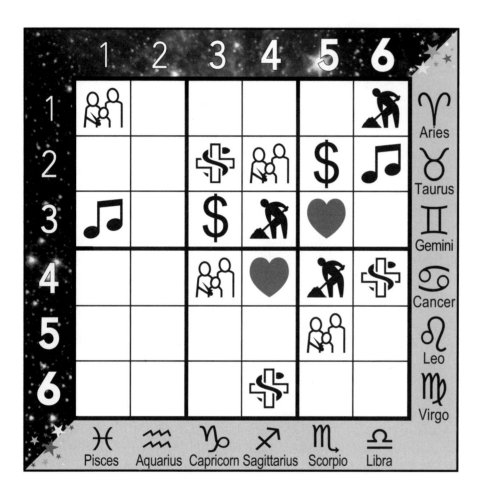

DOUBLETALK

What word means "to fasten together" or "to cut off"?

★ Futoshiki

Fill in the 5 x 5 grid with numbers 1 to 5 only once per row and column, while following the greater than/lesser than symbols shown. There is only one valid solution per puzzle that can be reached through logic and clear thinking alone!

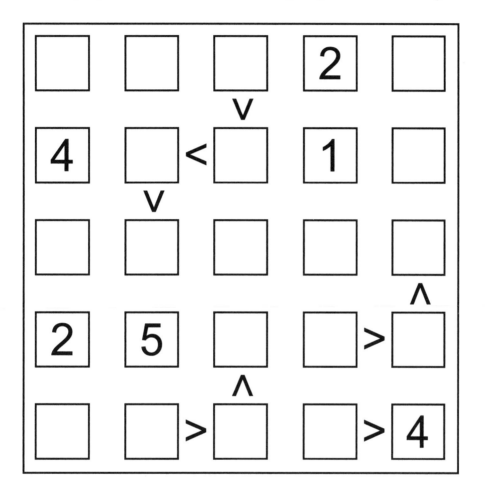

REPOSITION PREPOSITION

Unscramble OFTEN I SIP and find a triple word preposition.

★★★ Peewee League by Karen Peterson

ACROSS

1 Lacking spice
5 Chaplin persona
10 Giant in audio equipment
14 Cameo stone
15 They form central angles
16 A dash of panache
17 Hokkaido native
18 Harebrained
19 Happen across
20 2000 Woody Allen film
23 Exam taker
24 Gossip sheet
25 India tourism magnet
27 Unyoke oxen
31 *The Good Earth* setting
34 Chaney and Chaney, Jr.
36 Muslim general
37 *H.M.S. Pinafore* character
41 Corolla petal
42 Corrida snorter
43 Evenings, in ad-speak
44 1945 conference site
47 *Bonnie and Clyde* director
49 2001 boxing biopic
50 Endangered marine mammal
54 Shirley Temple film
60 Not one
61 Itty
62 Ill at ___ (uncomfortable)
63 Mold-ripened cheese
64 Cordelia's sister
65 P&L preparers
66 Mime
67 Amount of yarn
68 Cattle, formerly

DOWN

1 Occasion to stand up
2 Japanese cartoon
3 Chatty birds
4 Jubilant
5 More banal
6 Wife of rajah
7 Early rib donor
8 Colliery
9 Tart part
10 Renders unclear
11 Ragbag
12 Made a putt
13 Culminates
21 Kind of pad or tender
22 Mob target
26 *Tuesdays With Morrie* author
27 "___ of Old Smokey"
28 Peace conference result
29 Flulike symptom
30 Siestas
31 Thunderpeal
32 Panaewa Rainforest Zoo site
33 "Let's leave ___ that"
35 ___ *Mutual Friend*: Dickens
38 Digital sellers
39 World-weariness
40 Pheasant, for one
45 Finn's pal
46 551, to Caesar
48 Comedic actor in *Mary Poppins*
51 1900 zoological discovery
52 Seder month
53 Migratory birds
54 Los Angeles Sparks org.
55 Tombstone marshal
56 Canal of song
57 Soup plant
58 *Picnic* playwright
59 Morales in *Paid in Full*

★ Alpinism

All the words are hidden vertically, horizontally or diagonally—in both directions. The letters that remain unused form a sentence from left to right.

```
B U I K B R I D G I N G L D S
E R C I S N O P M A R C N G C
B O W L I N E K N O T U S U O
R U D A L L Y K I L C P L L R
E T N G A L O B E H L T I M E
C D A L I O A B I E N M A R B
I O M N H L T M G E G G G O G
G O M T A S N L M F N T H E E
A R O N I E O P X E I T E R H
L O C A Y O I I S O R R O F C
F E W S P U B I U I E L H D T
I N G S Q Q U I C K D R A W I
R O P E I M S L A N L E R W H
K M O U N T A I N S U E N S E
A N C H O R B E N D O X E C V
R O O D N I I S T I B X S N O
R E T T O P S B G H E Y S P L
W E R C S C R A S H P A D E C
```

CRAMPONS
CRASH PAD
EQUIPMENT
FLAG
FOOT HOOK
GRIP
HARNESS
HEXES
INDOOR
KNOTS
LEG LOOP
MAGNESIUM
MOUNTAINS
OUTDOOR
QUICKDRAW
ROCK
ROPE
SCORE
SCREW
SPOTTER
WAIST BELT

ABSEIL
ANCHOR BEND
BALANCE

BOULDERING
BOWLINE KNOT
BRIDGING

CHIMNEYS
CLOVE HITCH
COMMAND

TRANSADDITION

Add one letter to HUNT STAR FRINGES and rearrange the rest to find a connection.

★★ Sunny Weather

Where will the sun shine? With the knowledge that each arrow points to a place where a symbol should be, can you locate the sunny spots? The symbols cannot be next to each other vertically, horizontally or diagonally. A symbol cannot be placed on top of an arrow. We show one symbol.

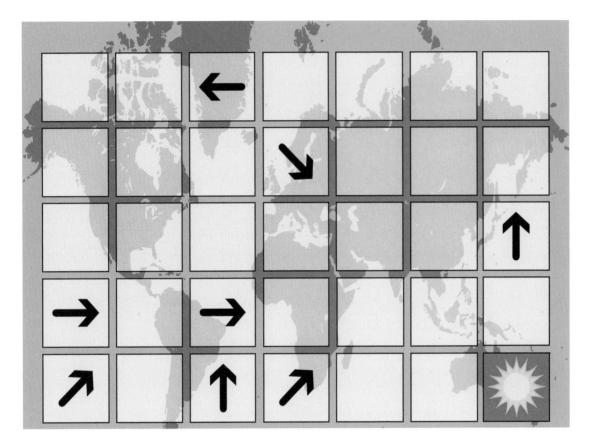

BLOCK ANAGRAM

Form the word that is described in the brackets with the letters above the grid. Extra letters are already in the right place.

BANKERS (U.S. State)

★★★ Punny and Funny II by Tim Wagner

ACROSS

1 Author Silverstein
5 Medieval fiddle
10 Stylist's creation
14 Cut corners
15 Hersey bell town
16 Guisado cooker
17 Lilting melodies
18 Burgundy grape
19 Inside the foul line
20 Santa in action?
23 Satellite of Uranus
24 "Right you ___!"
25 Affirmative reply
26 Insinuates
31 Rejuvenate
34 Seawater barrier
35 Alley-___
36 Rara ___
37 Tennis great Monica
38 Enjoying a lot
39 Sadie Hawkins Day catches
40 Milan opera house (with "La")
41 Metal brick
42 Part of a balanced diet
44 Six-legged queen
45 Travel through time?
46 Give credit to
50 One may do this on an Easter hunt?
55 Jai ___
56 County in Ireland
57 Sullen expression
58 Twice-told tale
59 Consumed
60 Memo line
61 Hosiery headache
62 Frozen rain
63 Tropical fruit

DOWN

1 Sudden contraction
2 West Indies republic
3 Glitch
4 Port of 2 Down
5 Raging waters
6 Monsoon of *Absolutely Fabulous*
7 Pistol pop
8 Seth's son
9 Cape Cod abodes
10 Morning mugful
11 *Lemony Snicket* evil count
12 Tennis rival of Bjorn
13 Jamie of *M*A*S*H*
21 Had the answer
22 Strongly advise
26 Nasdaq trades
27 Eye part
28 iTunes download
29 Revealer of Oz
30 Make out
31 Airport incline
32 At any time
33 Cuban boy
34 Low fat
37 Math and others
38 Courageous
40 Utah's lily
41 Part of a foot
43 "___ a Chance on Love"
44 Say yes
46 Jibe
47 *Silver Shark* novelist Andrews
48 Spill the beans
49 Socialite Lauder
50 Customs
51 Cumming in *Burlesque*
52 *Doctor Zhivago* heroine
53 Airline to Tel Aviv
54 Boarding site

★★ BrainSnack®—Write Me

In the letter below, what should be the fifth word underlined?

END GAME

The words you are seeking all have the letters END in them in the position indicated.
When you have found all of the answers, from the clues on the right, one column will reveal the
END GAME word which will give you something to enthuse about.

```
_ _ _ _ _ E N D       To shine brightly
_ _ _ E N D _ _        Attached
_ E N D _ _ _ _        Fit for sale
E N D _ _ _ _ _        Marriage within a particular group
```

★★ Kakuro

Each number in a black area is the sum of the numbers that you have to enter in the next empty boxes. The empty boxes that make up the sum are called a run. The sum of the across run is written above the diagonal in the black area and the sum of the down run is written below the diagonal. Runs can only contain the numbers 1 through 9 and each number in a run can only be used once. The gray boxes only contain odd numbers and the white only even numbers.

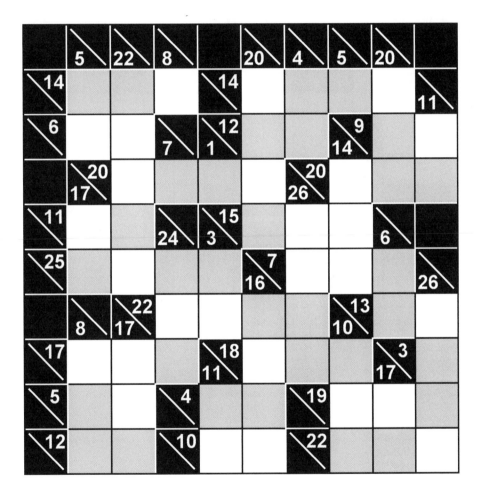

MISSING LETTER PROVERB

Fill in each missing letter, indicated by an X, to make a well-known proverb.

XOUTX IX XASTEX OX XHX XOUNX

★★★ P Soup by Don Law

ACROSS

1 Attend Exeter
5 Water collectors
10 Third place, at the track
14 Sitarist Shankar
15 Rainbow fish
16 Timbuktu's land
17 Something unique
18 Lightsome
19 Ruler of Valhalla
20 Part of a road test
23 Not a one
24 Anonymous John
25 Most luxurious
29 Father or brother
33 Corn lily
34 Gave flowers and candy to
36 Blood type system
37 He or she, e.g.
41 Cyclone center
42 Weather balloon
43 Irish Gaelic
44 Patronizing Netflix
46 Aussie sheepdogs
49 Yanks of 1917
50 Stan of Spider-Man fame
51 One making faces?
60 Part of QED
61 That is to say
62 Ocean motion
63 Hot item
64 Square things
65 Give careful attention to
66 Gland finale?
67 Zapped
68 White-tailed raptors

DOWN

1 Shore up
2 Frog genus
3 "Thanks ___ so much!"
4 Voracious fish
5 Stable units
6 Recommend
7 Dirty up
8 Cheesy fiction
9 Less wobbly
10 Camel pack?
11 "___ only known!"
12 Lena in *Chocolat*
13 Hockey position
21 Polygraph indication
22 Sonata section
25 Skirler
26 Daisy that's a weed
27 Firehouse feature
28 Guitar's sound

29 Fraction of a ruble
30 New Zealand native
31 Maltreatment
32 Date before ides
35 Aged
38 American dogwood
39 Survivable
40 Drink of forgetfulness
45 Torn shred
47 In hog heaven
48 Luau souvenir
51 Andean land
52 Like some medicines
53 Music of India
54 Minute amount
55 Deuces
56 Spruce relative
57 Stadium division
58 First place
59 Wine list section

★★ Word Sudoku

Complete the grid so that each row, each column and each 3 x 3 frame contains the nine letters from the black box below. The hidden nine-letter word is in the diagonal from top left to bottom right.

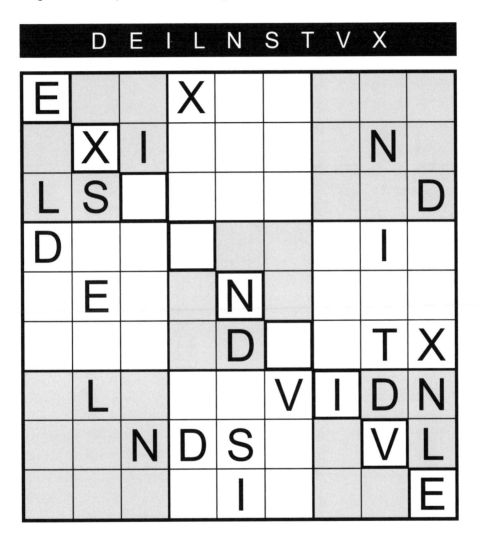

D E I L N S T V X

LETTERBLOCKS

Move the letterblocks around so that words are formed on top and below that you can associate with artists.

WRH * LAO
CAGLLHA

★★ Keep Going

Start on a blank square of your choice and connect as many blank squares as possible with one single continuous line. You can only connect squares along vertical and horizontal lines, not along diagonal lines. You must continue the connecting line up until the next obstacle, i.e., the rim of the box, a black square or a square that has already been used. You can change direction at any obstacle you meet. Each square can only be used once. The number of blank squares that will be left unused is marked in the upper square. There is more than one solution. We only show one solution.

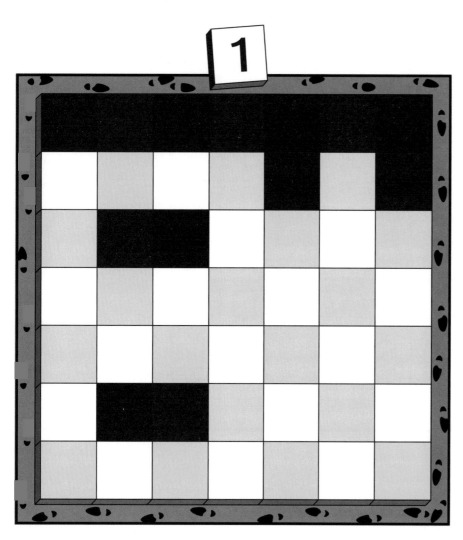

DELETE ONE

Delete one letter from THEM TOLD DO RHUBARB and rearrange the rest to find a nursery rhyme character.

★★★ It's About Time by John McCarthy

ACROSS

1 July 18, 1944 victory site
5 Short of
11 Chart
14 Not give ___ about
15 Tell a bedtime story
16 Crete's highest mountain
17 Is a hero
19 "I should say ___!"
20 Sails near the stern
21 Yuk it up
23 Olympus Mons location
24 Hair braid
26 How beavers work
29 Magnificence
32 Ameliorate
33 Where a stray may stay
34 Upstate NY school
35 Alphabet openers
36 Take to task
37 Bread served with falafel
38 ___-Magnon
39 How Lindy flew
40 Salad-bar bits
41 Postage and ___
43 "As if that ___ enough ..."
44 Phony duck
45 Kentucky Derby horse
46 "I'm so excited!"
48 First to arrive
52 Rudy's coach in *Rudy*
53 Egg timers
56 Ballroom dancer Goodman
57 Emulated Isocrates
58 *A Bug's Life* bug
59 Wee bit
60 Bottom berths
61 Proximal

DOWN

1 Cross talk?
2 Fairway hazard
3 Stromboli output
4 It's receptive to new ideas
5 Circulation conduit
6 Kiln relatives
7 Clarke and West
8 Kooky
9 Depot: Abbr.
10 *Babes in* ___ (1934)
11 Precooked grain product
12 Ouida's ___ *of Flanders*
13 Bikeway
18 Medieval poet
22 Help
24 Puritan
25 Highway section

26 Place for a boardwalk
27 Eclipse shadow
28 A watch may have a "sweep" one
29 Word repeated before "gone"
30 Pulitzer author Sinclair
31 Jolly
33 Imposter
36 TV commercials award
37 Follower
39 Booze
40 Kristen's *Twilight* role
42 ___ volente (God willing)
43 *War of the* ___ (2005)
45 Hoopster
46 Goofy creator
47 Polygonal calculation
48 Art deco notable

49 Sunrise location, in Sonora
50 Biological bristle
51 Romanov ruler
54 Conquistadore's loot
55 Detroit union

★★★ Sport Maze

Draw the shortest way from the ball to the goal. You can only move along vertical and horizontal lines, not along diagonal lines. The figure on each square indicates the number of squares the ball must be moved in the same direction. You can change direction at each stop.

0	3	3	3	1	4
1	4	3	2	1	4
1	2	3	1	2	4
1	2	1	0	1	
1	3	1	4	2	2
3	5	3	1	2	3

LETTER LINE

Put a letter in each of the squares below to make a word which means "a member of the Alcedinidae family." These numbered clues refer to other words which can be made from the whole.

4 10 2 9 5 SORROW; 8 2 3 4 9 JOINT; 5 10 2 7 1 QUICK SEARCH; 5 9 2 4 3 PRETEND.

1	2	3	4	5	6	7	8	9	10

★★★ Sudoku

Fill in the grid so that each row, each column and each 3 x 3 frame contains every number from 1 to 9.

		3	4	8	5	1		9
4			3					8
1								6
				9	6			
2			7	3		6		
	4		8			9		
3	7							5
		5						
8						4		

CHANGELINGS

Each of the three lines of letters below spell words which you could find in a kitchen, but the letters have been mixed up. Four letters from the first word are now in the third line, four letters from the third word are in the second line and four letters from the second word are in the first line. The remaining letters are in their original places. What are the words?

```
P E O P S T I O R S
B S R C O L A T P N
T A C L E H C O O K
```

★★★ BrainSnack®—History Tour

The historian has already visited castles A, B and C. Which castle (1–9) will he visit next?

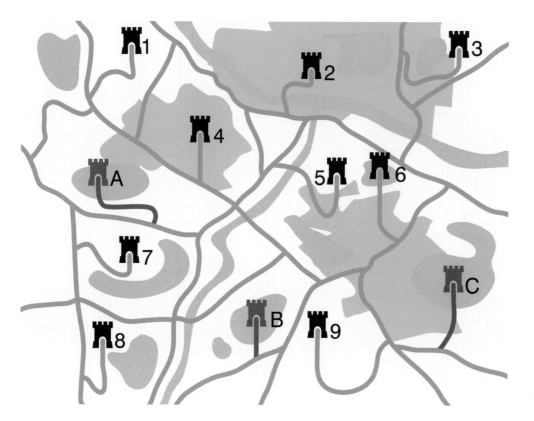

ONE LETTER LESS OR MORE

The word on the right side contains the letters of the word on the left side plus or minus the letter in the middle. One letter is already in the right place.

| E | I | N | S | T | E | I | N | +V | | | | | N | | | | |

★★★ Oxymorons I by Don Law

ACROSS

1 Weightlifter's powder
5 Musical Moore
10 Shower gel
14 Sundry collection
15 "___ ears!"
16 Friendly
17 Mariners
18 Turn off
19 Under sail
20 Industrious senior citizens
23 Type of manual
24 Tale of ___
25 Tribal doctor
28 Swimming kick
33 Skin cosmetic
34 Alda and Ladd
35 Quarterback Newton
36 Crafts
37 "That's ___ your head!"
38 Tibetan sighting
39 Amin of Uganda
40 Commencement
41 Extreme amount
42 May-___ romance
44 Steinway products
45 "Joyful Girl" singer DiFranco
46 Wolf's look
47 First findings
54 Moore in *A Few Good Men*
55 Canonization result
56 Gets annoying
58 *First Love* author Turgenev
59 Cheer greatly
60 Entre ___ (between us)
61 Pack
62 Grief
63 Little nuisance

DOWN

1 Kiddie
2 Winglike
3 Old money of Rome
4 Halloween wear
5 2006 Best Actress winner
6 Qatar biggie
7 Friday employer
8 Spent unwisely
9 Permissive
10 ___ *on a Plane* (2006)
11 Seine tributary
12 Green car in *Cars 2*
13 Round veggies
21 Munich's river
22 Billionaire Perot
25 Straitlaced
26 Pack
27 Bit of impishness
28 More like a fox

29 "___ Buy Me Love": Beatles
30 It has arms and waves
31 *Midnight Cowboy* antihero
32 Jimmy in *Star Wars Episode III*
34 South African fox
37 Fair-minded
38 Horse that isn't two yet
40 Prefix for potent
41 Substitute position
43 Out to lunch
44 Bother
46 Direction for a funeral march
47 "Got it, daddy-o!"
48 St. Petersburg river
49 Model wife of David Bowie

50 *Le Roi d'Ys* composer
51 Omani money
52 2010 Disney sci-fi film
53 Arctic bird
57 Former British Airways jet

★ Literature

All the words are hidden vertically, horizontally or diagonally—in both directions. The letters that remain unused form a sentence from left to right.

```
P  L  I  T  E  R  A  E  L  R  Y  A  U  T  H
O  O  P  L  O  T  P  L  E  G  E  N  D  R  S
E  W  A  N  T  I  T  Y  V  Y  A  S  S  E  B
M  O  P  C  C  N  O  R  O  M  Y  X  O  A  O
P  F  C  A  N  O  N  I  N  O  V  E  L  L  A
N  O  I  V  R  E  Y  C  L  A  M  L  E  S  S
D  U  E  C  A  O  L  A  A  Y  A  G  E  W  T
W  I  A  T  T  I  D  L  N  D  I  T  H  N  R
F  E  A  E  B  I  T  Y  O  E  H  E  E  I  A
A  S  I  R  D  R  O  T  I  M  M  M  E  X  V
I  T  A  V  Y  N  T  N  G  O  H  Y  M  N  E
R  R  L  S  E  I  O  N  E  C  A  N  T  A  L
Y  U  L  M  R  R  O  R  R  O  H  T  I  H  S
T  C  E  O  M  E  T  A  P  H  O  R  S  T  T
A  T  G  T  I  C  P  T  E  K  C  O  P  P  O
L  U  O  I  M  C  R  I  T  I  Q  U  E  L  R
E  R  R  F  A  N  E  T  O  D  C  E  N  A  Y
N  E  Y  S  C  I  T  A  M  A  R  D  E  Y  R
```

DIARY
DRAMATICS
EPIC
ESSAY
FAIRY TALE
FICTION
HORROR
HYMN
LEGEND
LIBRARY
LYRICAL
METAPHOR
MOTIF
MYTH
NOVELLA
OXYMORON
PARCHMENT
PARODY
PLAY
PLOT
POCKET
POEM
POET
REGIONAL NOVEL
REVIEW
RONDEAU
STRUCTURE
TRAVEL STORY

ALLEGORY   BALLAD   COMEDY
ANECDOTE   CANON   CRITIQUE

UNCANNY TURN

Rearrange the letters of the phrase to form a cognate anagram, one which is related or connected in meaning to the original phrase. The answer can be one or more words.

TRY POE

★★★ BrainSnack®—Weigh it Up

Which weight between 1 and 10 grams cannot be weighed with the three available weights using only one weighing?

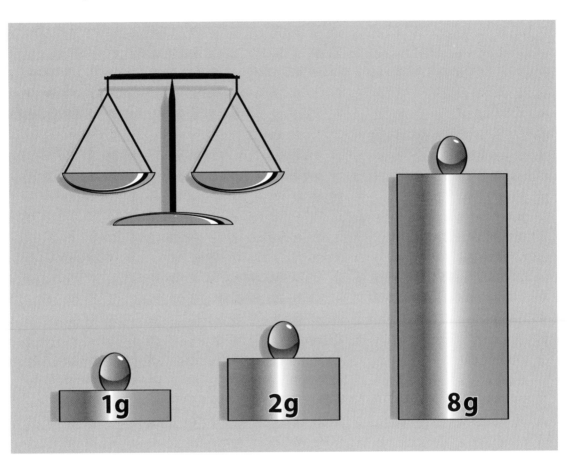

DOODLE PUZZLE

A doodle puzzle is a combination of images, letters and/or numbers that represent a word or a concept. If you cannot solve a doodle puzzle, do not look at the answer right away. Think hard—and outside the box.

★★★ Oxymorons II by Don Law

ACROSS
1 Ungulate feature
5 Gem weight
10 Like Santa's bag on Christmas Eve
14 MMX or MXM, e.g.
15 Photoshop company
16 Descendant of a crumhorn
17 Grandpa Walton portrayer
18 Royal crown
19 Dark wines
20 How to keep a debate friendly
23 Varlets
24 Siding with
25 Peer Gynt's mother
26 Two-wheelers
31 Squirming
34 Flatware item
35 Coolidge or Ripken
36 Thai money
37 Make butter
38 Sit before a lens
39 Kyushu volcano
40 Nordic natural wonder
41 Orange juice preference
42 Undergrads
44 PETA's pet peeve
45 Poetic dusk
46 Write music
50 Making waves, e.g.?
55 Invisible quality
56 Corday's victim
57 Utters
58 "___ Old Cowhand"
59 Deliver a keynote
60 Magazine for the fashion-conscious
61 Ultimate
62 Consumer advocate Ralph
63 Observed

DOWN
1 Viking of comics
2 Russian lake
3 Unrivaled individuals
4 Predict
5 Roundup group
6 "So long, señor!"
7 Kind of rage
8 Dugout shelter
9 Sugar measure
10 Drew a blank
11 Slang prefix meaning "super"
12 Bonanza vein
13 ___ majesty
21 "Not so fast!"
22 Elvis ___ Presley
26 San Antonio NBA team
27 Big stack of firewood
28 Park concern: Abbr.

29 Scratchy voice
30 Loom part
31 Arab garments
32 Boss Tweed lampooner
33 Old pronoun
34 Got the picture
37 Spice made from bark
38 Reasons
40 Yard sections
41 Low-cut shoe
43 Pour into a carafe, say
44 "O Susanna" composer
46 Orange box
47 Alb coverer
48 Vogue
49 Ruhr region
50 Hoist the main
51 Deer enemy
52 Historic periods
53 Figure skater Lipinski
54 Toward the mouth

★ Wind Instruments

All the words are hidden vertically, horizontally or diagonally—in both directions. The letters that remain unused form a sentence from left to right.

```
E M O U T H P I E C E A B R C
L A T L R E S O N A T O R S L
G S E B O A R E D R O C E R A
U B P N D C I S A N O E E N R
B R M S S E C M B L L H E I I
T E U H V E A I T P C O A N N
N A R S I A P S P T M S O A E
O T T F B R L I A S S U B S T
I H C T I P F V P Y P U S L A
R I Y E R S A N E N T D P I E
A N R C U S S K I S A O E N C
L G M U I N O M R A H P P P O
C S S I B L A C C O R D I O N
Y F D I D G E R I D O O P S U
P L I P S N P L E M E N G T E
D U W I T H U A E M U L A H C
S T A X O P N O I T A R B I V
H E O N E A R T S E H C R O S
```

FIPPLE
FLUTE
HARMONIUM
HORN
KEYS
LIPS
MOUTHPIECE
MUSIC
ORCHESTRA
PANPIPES
PICCOLO
PITCH
RECORDER
RESONATOR
SOUND
TRUMPET
TUBA
VALVES
VIBRATION

ACCORDION
AIR
BAGPIPE

BREATHING
BUGLE
CHALUMEAU

CLARINET
CLARION
DIDGERIDOO

CHANGE ONE

Change one letter in each of these two words to form a common two-word phrase.

BANDS DAWN

★ Safe Code

To open the safe you have to replace the question marks with the correct figures. You can find these figures by determining the logical methods behind the numbers shown. These methods may include calculation, inversion, repetition, chronological succession, forming ascending and descending series.

SAFE A08

DOODLE PUZZLE

A doodle puzzle is a combination of images, letters and/or numbers that represent a word or a concept. If you cannot solve a doodle puzzle, do not look at the answer right away. Think hard—and outside the box.

★★★ Oxymorons III by Don Law

ACROSS

1 Dog-paddle
5 Competed at Pimlico
10 Cribbage pins
14 Leaning Tower of ___
15 Qatar's ruler
16 O.K. Corral lawman
17 Month in Tel Aviv
18 Showy lily
19 Like ___ of sunshine
20 Like gallows humor?
23 Shows one's humanity
24 Capote, briefly
25 Joins an ice show
28 Dew
33 Summit goals
34 ___ cum laude
35 Style guru Gunn
36 Hershfield hero
37 French market town
38 Sherlockian trademark
39 Part of TGIF
40 Cut a sandwich, say
41 "If I Only Had a Brain" composer
42 Stumbling block
44 Recommended reply to a sentry
45 Regal letters
46 Caught sight of
47 Tutor in training
54 Housing for seniors?
55 Mooed
56 Gutter locale
57 Reynolds film *Rent-___*
58 Nana Oyl's daughter
59 Tried to touch base
60 "The ___ the limit!"
61 Pilot's "OK"
62 Millennium Falcon pilot

DOWN

1 Hydrotherapy havens
2 Expansive
3 River to the Danube
4 Hartley in *1969*
5 Comes back, as a dream
6 Build up in a heap
7 Stephen King novel
8 Hard to catch
9 Tailgating, Indy-style
10 M&M's variety
11 Take home, as pay
12 Squirrel color
13 Smart or Smiley
21 Metal containers?
22 Constellation bear
25 Wolfgang Puck eatery
26 Meal on a skewer
27 Base neutralizers
28 Purple dye
29 Nasty brute
30 Not merely decorative
31 Become mature
32 Revise a text
34 Gangster gal
37 James Buchanan was one
38 Cinderella became one
40 No piece of cake
41 Territory
43 Sounds of an excited heart
44 Birdbath companion
46 McQueen or Martin
47 Simple puppet
48 *Troilus and Cressida* setting
49 ___ contendere
50 Bit of a nest
51 Corona
52 Nefarious
53 Makeover
54 ___ *Rheingold*

★★ Keep Going

Start on a blank square of your choice and connect as many blank squares as possible with one single continuous line. You can only connect squares along vertical and horizontal lines, not along diagonal lines. You must continue the connecting line up until the next obstacle, i.e., the rim of the box, a black square or a square that has already been used. You can change direction at any obstacle you meet. Each square can only be used once. The number of blank squares that will be left unused is marked in the upper square. There is more than one solution. We only show one solution.

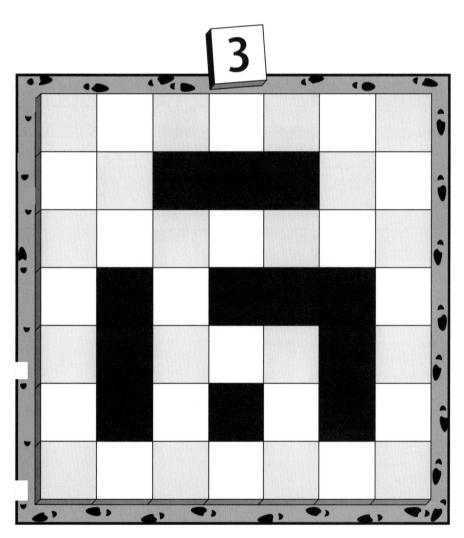

FRIENDS

What do the following words have in common?

CLOSE SEE BEAR CAST FINGER GO LEG LOCK

★ Word Sudoku

Complete the grid so that each row, each column and each 3 x 3 frame contains the nine letters from the black box below. The hidden nine-letter word is in the diagonal from top left to bottom right.

A I J L N O Q S T

I		Q		T	A			L
		T	I				N	
	N				Q		J	
Q			L	N	S			
N					I			
	L	A			T			
			J				L	T
	Q					S		
					A			

SANDWICH

What four-letter word belongs between the word at left and the word at right, so that the first and second word, and the second and third word, each form a common compound word or phrase?

PASS _ _ _ _ GAME

★★★ Fictional High Schools by John M. Samson

ACROSS

1 Shell game
5 Not easily excitable
10 Hand (out)
14 "Time" singer Amos
15 Orange Bowl city
16 Manipulator
17 Something for the poor
18 Gather logically
19 Hindu wrap
20 *Saved by the Bell* high school
22 *Veronica Mars* high school
24 *Swan Lake* step
25 Premier Zhu's successor
26 Printer's primary color
30 Regulate
34 Form of ether
35 Irritant in one's side
37 "The ___ Daba Honeymoon"
38 *Glee* high school
42 Leary's trip ticket
43 Camel relative
44 In a different manner
45 Class period
47 Paint gun
50 Tennis trophy
51 Joint owners' pronoun
52 *The Breakfast Club* high school
56 *My So-Called Life* high school
60 Growing group
61 Abe Lincoln's birthplace
63 Invisible radiation
64 Kind of presentation
65 Torpid
66 Kind of shovel
67 Telephone inventor
68 Travel reference
69 Danson and Turner

DOWN

1 Fork
2 Fizzy drink
3 Part of *M*A*S*H*
4 Write "seperately," say
5 In the hub of
6 Checkout queue
7 Fool
8 Preindication
9 2010 Katy Perry song
10 Ought not
11 Isaac's firstborn
12 Sea swallow
13 Lake Amerind
21 Fleming or Paisley
23 Coin of Finland
26 Whimpers
27 Absinthe flavoring
28 First-place medals
29 Hindu oversoul
30 Andean shrubs
31 Pregame rah-rah meeting
32 Way past fat
33 Kind of cake
36 "Let me think ..."
39 Hipbone
40 Baldness
41 Saudi Arabia locale
46 Dead Sea artifact
48 Indicates direction
49 Difficulty
52 Snooty sort
53 Lagomorph
54 "There are more names ..."
55 Aggressive oratory
56 Coin in Trevi Fountain
57 Letter used by Odin
58 Stepped along
59 Fishtails
62 ___ Paese cheese

★★★ Sport Maze

Draw the shortest way from the ball to the goal. You can only move along vertical and horizontal lines, not along diagonal lines. The figure on each square indicates the number of squares the ball must be moved in the same direction. You can change direction at each stop.

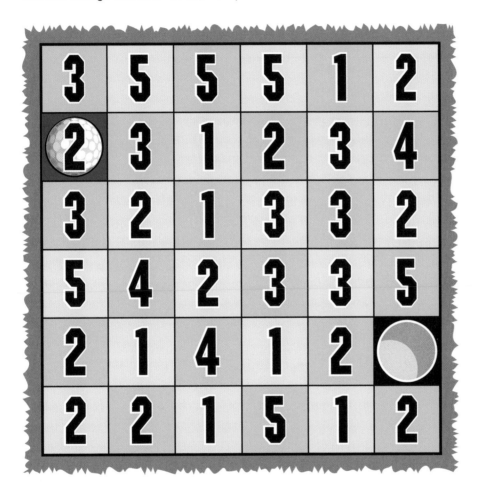

LETTERBLOCKS

Move the letterblocks around so that words are formed on top and below that you can associate with business.

★★ Sudoku X

Fill in the grid so that each row, each column and each 3 x 3 frame contains every number from 1 to 9. The two main diagonals of the grid also contain every number from 1 to 9.

		9	4	1		7	6	3
				5	2			
	7		3	9	5	2	8	
2		5		4		8	6	
7		1		3	2	5		
1			9			4		
			6	5				
					8	1	5	

REPOSITION PREPOSITION

Unscramble CANOE FLIP and find a triple word preposition.

★★★ Wordplay by Peggy O'Shea

ACROSS

1 Killer whale
5 Central point
10 It's a lot if it's a lot
14 Batting material
15 Set things square
16 Small building
17 Digital workout
20 Like the B-2 bomber
21 "Horsefeathers!"
22 201, in old Rome
23 Indy 500 entrant
24 Name to a post
28 It may prompt a quarantine
32 A-Rod's base
33 Third rock from the Sun
35 After-school org.
36 Muscle quality
37 Chicago mayor in 2010
38 Groundbreaking discoveries?
39 Figure skater Midori
40 "Hasta la ___, baby!"
41 Church top
42 Not verbose
44 Spotted
46 Dada sculptor
47 Dove sound
48 Hermione of Hogwarts
52 Bishop's staff
56 You can never bank on it?
58 Nameless, briefly
59 At ___ and sevens
60 Mackerel gull
61 Use a doormat
62 Puts in a good word?
63 Latin infinitive

DOWN

1 Holds title to
2 Sound defeat
3 Obey a summons
4 Bluefin relative
5 Chris of Coldplay
6 Seven-year malady
7 June beetle
8 Cold-shoulder
9 Stick-to-it-iveness
10 On land
11 Facial part that's stroked
12 Actor Auberjonois
13 Irritable
18 "Champion" of Spanish history
19 Cymbal sound
24 *La Bohème* setting
25 Passport feature
26 Nut pine
27 Comb the "wrong" way
28 Fearful feeling
29 Shakespeare's birth month
30 Cubic meter
31 Lightened up
34 Key below Z
37 Allocate
38 Night, to day
40 Late summer sign
41 Reel
43 Baboon tooth
45 Crossword direction
48 Tackle a bone
49 *Doctor Who* villainess
50 Above it all
51 Worry for a speakeasy patron
52 Friend of Frank and Joe Hardy
53 March 15
54 Teacup handles
55 Hall-of-Famer Sandberg
57 61

★★★ BrainSnack®—Symbolism

Which symbol (1-6) should replace the question mark?

DOUBLETALK

What word means "to secure in place" or "to dash away suddenly"?

★ Word Pyramid

Each word in the pyramid has the letters of the word above it, plus a new letter.

E

(1) Exist
(2) Unit of sound intensity equal to 10 decibels
(3) Capable
(4) Piece of furniture
(5) Horse barn
(6) Conflicts
(7) Used in a car or plane to hold you in your seat

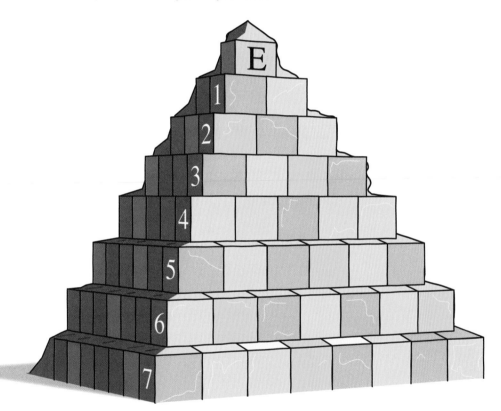

TRANSADDITION

Add one letter to MEASUREMENT and rearrange the rest to find a connection.

★★ Sunny Weather

Where will the sun shine? With the knowledge that each arrow points to a place where a symbol should be, can you locate the sunny spots? The symbols cannot be next to each other vertically, horizontally or diagonally. A symbol cannot be placed on top of an arrow. We show one symbol.

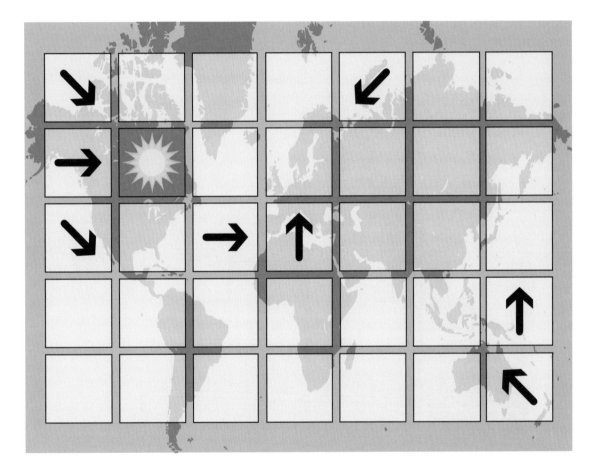

BLOCK ANAGRAM

Form the word that is described in the brackets with the letters above the grid. An extra letter is already in the right place.

ICE BLISTER (widely known persons)

★★★★ More Wordplay by Peggy O'Shea

ACROSS

1 Aware of
5 It grows in the dark
10 Open, but barely
14 Picasso's room
15 Do more than apologize
16 James in *Only When I Laugh*
17 Invectives from the aft?
20 Backslide
21 Very vivid
22 Philippine volcano
23 Coffee tank
24 Highland plaids
28 Wordsmiths
32 Projecting window design
33 Ancient Roman senate
35 Wimbledon champ Seixas
36 Be inclined (to)
37 Blanches
38 Cleave
39 Some spaces
40 Taxonomic category
41 Candy nut
42 *She Done Him Wrong* star
44 Prickly plant
46 Echidna's morsel
47 Shady Tolkien creature
48 Isherwood's *The Berlin* ___
52 One of the Bee Gees
56 Note from Leo Burnett?
58 "Let's shake ___!"
59 "Guitar Town" singer Steve
60 "Small world, ___ it?"
61 Alongside of
62 Profound fear
63 Memo

DOWN

1 Stalin's empire
2 Chopped liver dish
3 Russian skater Protopopov
4 Did some voice-over work
5 Anglican preacher
6 SUVs
7 Soda
8 Cross letters
9 *Trinity* author
10 Stress
11 Dr. Dolittle
12 "Pocket rockets" in poker
13 Stage mom in *Gypsy*
18 Kathmandu locale
19 Heart parts
24 Pole carving
25 Orlando's Amway ___
26 Wash lightly
27 Hardly any
28 Gain by force
29 Give the boot
30 Beau number two
31 *CSI* center
34 Knife for Nanook
37 Wouldn't leave be
38 Hold back
40 Wish granter
41 Centerfold
43 Creature comfort
45 Off the disabled list
48 Garbage boat
49 Collette in *Little Miss Sunshine*
50 Bypass
51 Harry Potter ID mark
52 Powers in *The Storm Rider*
53 ___ facto
54 Wheatback coin
55 "Symphony in Black" artist
57 Rancor

★ Sudoku Twin

Fill in the grid so that each row, each column and each 3 x 3 frame contains every number from 1 to 9. A sudoku twin is two connected 9 x 9 sudokus.

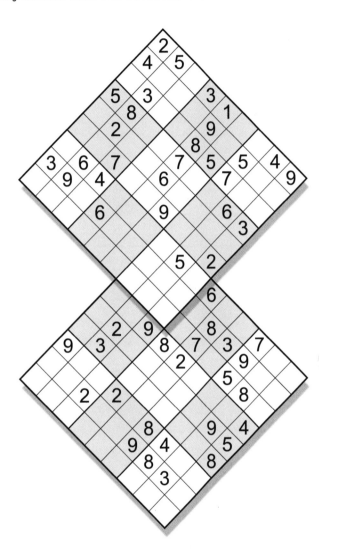

MISSING LETTER PROVERB

Fill in each missing letter, indicated by an X, to make a well-known proverb.

AXL TXIXGX XOMX XO TXOXE XXO XXIT

★ Futoshiki

Fill in the 5 x 5 grid with numbers 1 to 5 only once per row and column, while following the greater than/lesser than symbols shown. There is only one valid solution per puzzle that can be reached through logic and clear thinking alone!

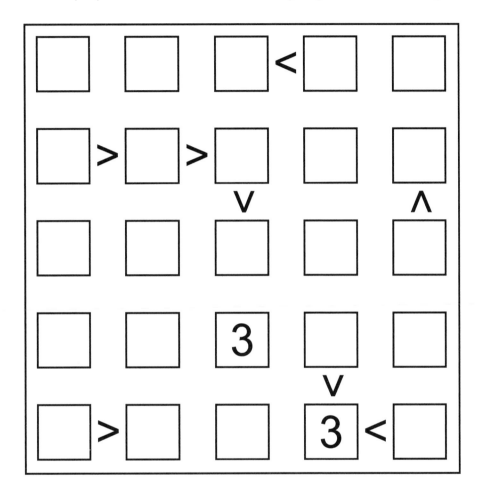

END GAME

The words you are seeking all have the letters END in them in the position indicated.
When you have found all of the answers, from the clues on the right, one column will reveal the END GAME word which will gradually disappear.

_ _ _ _ **E N D** _ _	Upset
_ _ _ _ **E N D**	Climb again
E N D _ _ _ _ _	Not the stated payee
_ _ **E N D** _ _ _	Continual

★★★★ Screen Legends Said by John M. Samson

ACROSS

1 Consequently
5 *Romeo and Juliet* et al.
10 Wooley in *Hoosiers*
14 Sign of decay
15 *Network* director
16 Tel Aviv dance
17 *Casablanca* heroine
18 Maternal relative
19 Big-budget film
20 "I never enjoyed working in a film": source
23 Tennis do-over
24 Curtail
25 Keene of Nancy Drew books
29 After the fact
33 Shangri-las
34 Toughen by exposure
36 Sugar suffix
37 Not on tape
38 Balsa vessels
39 Place Sundance liked
40 Wide shoe's letters
41 ___-burly
42 Whey-faced
43 Ammo
45 Renters
47 Lyricist Gershwin
48 Depot: Abbr.
49 "Big girls need big diamonds": source
58 Sarah Brightman, e.g.
59 Entrance courts
60 Captive of Hercules
61 Ways away
62 Culpability
63 Snowmobile
64 Patch up
65 Stadium path
66 New Mexico art colony

DOWN

1 Shipshape
2 Hawaiian skirt
3 Cold War superpower
4 *The Expendables* director
5 Oodles
6 Moon over Paris
7 *Diary of ___ Black Woman* (2005)
8 Sherpa bugaboo
9 2009 Super Bowl winners
10 Himalayan porter
11 Pueblo sun god
12 Rocker Burdon
13 One of the Three B's of music
21 Sushi seafood
22 Enameled metalware
25 Star

26 Bye-bye, in Burgundy
27 Paint the town red
28 Approaches
29 Inner tube rubber
30 Chilled ___ bone
31 Chandler or Lauder
32 College VIPs
35 Org. for 9 Down
38 Swedish turnip
39 Emerson, notably
41 Greek equivalent of Juno
42 *The Thin Man* dog
44 Chameleon, e.g.
46 Demesne
49 Netherlands cheese
50 Prison sentence
51 Cyclist Basso
52 Sewing case
53 Speaker of baseball
54 Sledding site

55 Germany's Oscar
56 Bread spread
57 Warren Beatty film

★★★ BrainSnack®—Carnival

Which two letters are missing in the conversation between the two Venetian carnival merrymakers?

DOODLE PUZZLE

A doodle puzzle is a combination of images, letters and/or numbers that represent a word or a concept. If you cannot solve a doodle puzzle, do not look at the answer right away. Think hard—and outside the box.

★ The Spy Who Came in From the Cold

The Puzzled Librarian was so busy fixing THE GOOD READS notice board, that she didn't see the stranger hovering beside the old card index files. The stranger pulled up a chair in front of them and took a piece of microfilm from his pocket and peered at it, holding it up to the light, then started to re-arrange the labels on the card index drawers. There is a message to be decoded. These numbers were on the microfilm:

7, 13, 1, 23, 2, 26, 11, 15, 5, 4, 16, 20, 30, 27, 18, 6, 8, 3, 12, 10, 19, 28, 9, 29, 22, 25, 24, 17, 21, 14.

LETTER LINE

Put a letter in each of the squares below to make a word which means "study through excavation and analysis." These numbered clues refer to other words which can be made from the whole.

1 2 10 11 8 6 A DIAMOND SHAPED PATTERN; 4 7 9 2 1 11 CHEER; 7 2 1 3 8 6 SOURCE OF ADVICE; 4 6 5 8 CURE.

1	2	3	4	5	6	7	8	9	10	11

★★★★ Presidents Cup—U.S.A. by Tim Wagner

ACROSS

1 2011 Presidents Cup golfer
5 On the ball
10 Do without
14 To be, in French class
15 Synagogue scroll
16 Latvian capital
17 Shrinking sea of Asia
18 Black wood
19 Living legend
20 2011 Presidents Cup golfer
22 Gumbo pod
23 Homo sapiens, e.g.
24 *Spamalot* creator Eric
26 Danson of *CSI*
27 Single guy
31 Cuban leader
34 Windows font
35 Road sign
36 Laundry unit
37 Mini
38 Churn up
39 Off-road vehicle
40 Preppy jackets
41 Lane in a Beatles song
42 Denied
44 Goldilocks was found in one
45 Judge
46 Otitis
50 Spy Hari
52 2011 Presidents Cup golfer
55 Ancient lyre
56 University founder Yale
57 ___ de force
58 Hammock support
59 In the sticks
60 Noted *Harper's Bazaar* artist
61 Child's play
62 Tuscany city
63 Owner's certificate

DOWN

1 Track trials
2 Anchors aweigh position
3 O'Hara's ___ *to Live*
4 Picked
5 Drunk as a skunk
6 Freight train hoppers
7 Ending with buck
8 Cape Town coin
9 Touchy-feely
10 Camden Yards bird
11 2011 Presidents Cup golfer
12 *The Munsters* bat
13 River to the Indian Ocean
21 Cambodian currency
25 Global shipping company
27 Rancher's mark
28 Is bedbound
29 *Chocolat* actress Lena
30 ___-poly
31 Jolly Roger, for one
32 Teensy bit
33 2011 Presidents Cup golfer
34 "Help," in Tours
37 Stutters
38 Edited
40 112.5 degrees heading
41 Home to El Misti volcano
43 At hand
44 Scott in *American Beauty*
46 *Fargo* producer Coen
47 A piece of work
48 ___ cuisine
49 Goofed
50 Lion with a mane
51 Global area
53 His, in Caen
54 Pirelli product

★★ Keep Going

Start on a blank square of your choice and connect as many blank squares as possible with one single continuous line. You can only connect squares along vertical and horizontal lines, not along diagonal lines. You must continue the connecting line up until the next obstacle, i.e., the rim of the box, a black square or a square that has already been used. You can change direction at any obstacle you meet. Each square can only be used once. The number of blank squares that will be left unused is marked in the upper square. There is more than one solution. We only show one solution.

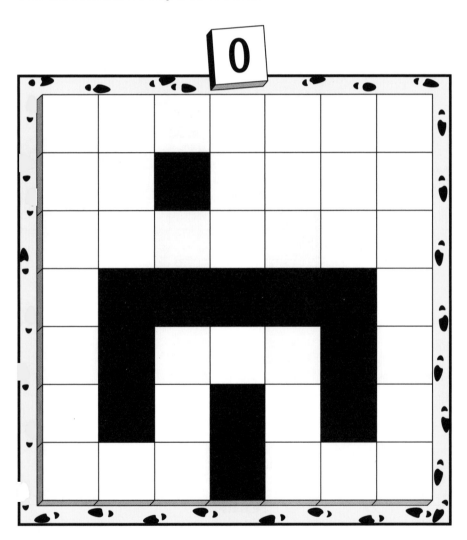

DELETE ONE

Delete one letter from UTOPIANS PITCH and rearrange the rest to find a tasty nibble.

★ Environment

All the words are hidden vertically, horizontally or diagonally—in both directions. The letters that remain unused form a sentence from left to right.

```
C O N S E R V A T I O N D E E
E R U T L U C I R G A G E C R
R A I N F O R E S T O V R O O
D A N G E R O U S A E R E L S
N S O L A R P A N E L N G O I
O T O Y K M E I N T S A N G O
I R N D S O M M C I A L A Y N
S O A N U A F H A O R G D A N
E P I Z L Y G R E N E D N I W
P E A S T T I O N A U S E A T
O R T E I M P T T O L R P R O
L T E D T C N I T X E T E C T
L T E H N O I T A R D Y H E D
U S U S T A I N A B L E E A E
T N F U N C T I O N A L V R I
I L I G H T P O L L U T I O N
O R O N G N I L C Y C E R L M
N E N O Z O N E L A Y E R F T
```

ENDANGERED
EROSION
EXTINCT
FAUNA
FLORA
FUNCTIONAL
HEALTH
KYOTO
LIGHT POLLUTION
MANURE
NOISE POLLUTION
OZONE LAYER
RAIN FOREST
RECYCLING
REPORT
SOLAR PANEL
SUSTAINABLE
TIDES
WIND ENERGY

AGRICULTURE
ANIMALS

CONSERVATION
DANGEROUS

DEHYDRATION
ECOLOGY

ONE LETTER LESS OR MORE

The word on the right side contains the letters of the word on the left side plus or minus the letter in the middle. One letter is already in the right place.

G E N E R A T E +M G ☐ ☐ ☐ ☐ ☐ ☐ ☐

★★★★ Directors Said by John M. Samson

ACROSS

1 Hole makers
5 Rough sketch
10 Wide-spreading trees
14 Stew vegetable
15 Fuel ship
16 Floor model
17 Roman 1052
18 Florida orange center
19 Andean ancient
20 "Drama is life with the dull bits cut out": source
23 Word form for "bad"
24 Toddler
25 Said one's lessons
29 Bow down before
33 Store up
34 Millennium's 1,000
36 ___ pro nobis
37 Supersonic speed unit
38 Pharmacy stock
39 For men only
40 Casino area
41 Related to the kidneys
42 Where the action is
43 On the skids
45 Like romantic nights
47 "Disgusting!"
48 Fjord cousin
49 "I dream for a living": source
58 Elbe tributary
59 *Silver Shark* novelist Andrews
60 Skullcap's lack
61 Frosty coat
62 Kind of hockey
63 Needlepoint fabric
64 Forcibly dislodge
65 Thompson and Samms
66 English prep school

DOWN

1 *Brokeback Mountain* heroine
2 Place for wishing
3 Explorer Ericson
4 Minor battle
5 Scribble
6 High in calories
7 Jai ___
8 Pool table cloth
9 Farm vehicles
10 Public notices
11 Letterman's rival
12 Nero's 2200
13 Linger in the hot tub
21 Chuckwagon offerings
22 ___ d'oeuvre
25 Highway exits
26 Electronic message
27 Flora in the Mojave
28 Faulkner's *As I Lay* ___
29 "If these ___ could talk ..."
30 "Monopoly" purchase
31 Native of Tabriz
32 Brewster of *Criminal Minds*
35 Guido's note
38 Whittling tool
39 Board game with letters
41 Risotto ingredient
42 Participate in America's Cup
44 Detour
46 Sneaker bottoms
49 Manhattan art gallery district
50 "How Great ___ Art"
51 Years of note
52 Willowy
53 "The Bells" is one
54 *Lost ___ Mancha* (2002)
55 Part of QED
56 Puerto ___
57 FBI agents

★★★ Sport Maze

Draw the shortest way from the ball to the goal. You can only move along vertical and horizontal lines, not along diagonal lines. The figure on each square indicates the number of squares the ball must be moved in the same direction. You can change direction at each stop.

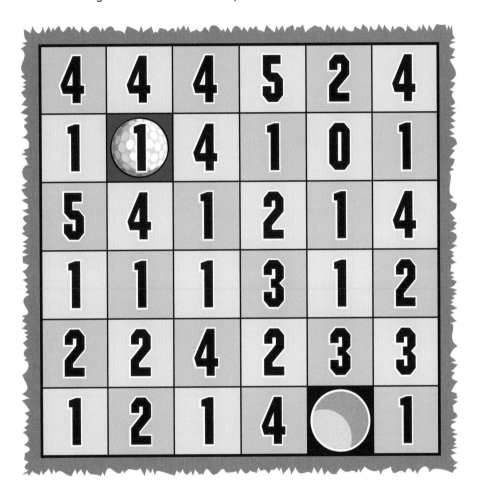

UNCANNY TURN

Rearrange the letters of the phrase to form a cognate anagram, one which is related or connected in meaning to the original phrase. The answer can be one or more words.

UP CLOSE

★★★★ Presidents Cup—International by Tim Wagner

ACROSS

1 One doing impressions
5 Off-the-cuff remark
10 Taj Mahal site
14 Prefix with scope
15 Hindu trinity member
16 Given by
17 Word after he and she
18 Encrypted
19 Cabinet face-lift
20 2011 Presidents Cup golfer
22 Important periods
23 Cannes movie house
24 Take hold
26 Ridiculous
29 Cruet contents
32 Twin crystal
33 Made a choice
34 Chromatin component
35 Dull pain
36 Dental filling
37 Self-satisfied
38 Mrs. bear
39 Like the Indian elephant
40 Blinding light
41 Photobucket upload
43 *A Few Good Men* director
44 Pitcher's mound bag
45 Salve
46 Catcher's glove
48 2011 Presidents Cup golfer
52 Thick goo
53 Easy ___
55 Aussie leaper
56 Wilson in *Midnight in Paris*
57 Charlie Bucket's friend
58 Gush forth
59 Shaker contents
60 "... ___ of skimble-skamble stuff": Shak.
61 Lick and stick

DOWN

1 Church recess
2 Tree for a partridge
3 Activist Brockovich
4 Mock
5 Balloon up
6 Asian wild dog
7 Kettle covers
8 "___ Got My Eyes on You"
9 2011 Presidents Cup golfer
10 Shaking in one's shoes
11 2011 Presidents Cup captain
12 Cabbed it
13 "Winter" singer Tori
21 Tipperary locale
24 Darkness Prince
25 Dollop
26 Stockpile
27 Side with eggs
28 2011 Presidents Cup golfer
29 Hitting sound
30 Make accustomed to
31 Amber ale
33 Salsa ingredient
36 2011 Presidents Cup golfer
37 Model quality
39 Pack animal
40 1996 Peace Prize Nobelist
42 Packing a wallop
43 Varlet
45 Rum cake
46 Jersey sounds
47 Home of the Hawkeyes
48 Miss Marple
49 Trick
50 Region
51 Mournful cry
54 Turf

★ Spot the Differences

Find the nine differences in the image on the right.

CHANGE ONE

Change one letter in each of these two words to form a common two-word phrase.

GLUE BEANS

★★★ Sudoku

Each row, column and 3 x 3 frame should contain every number from 1 to 9.

		4			1			3
8	5	3		7		6		
			6					
2				5			4	7
			8		2		9	
					5		6	9
		7					3	
			1	9	4			2

SQUIRCLES

Place consonants in the squares and vowels in the circles and form words in each vertical column. The definitions of the words you are looking for are listed.(The grid will reveal two geometrical shapes)

(1) Choice
(2) Words of a song
(3) Builds
(4) A base for art
(5) Appear
(6) Reflector
(7) Arrival of something important
(8) Help

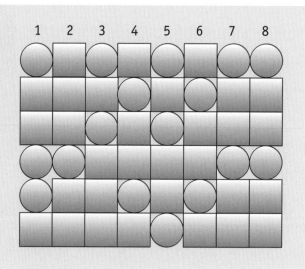

★★★ Word Sudoku

Complete the grid so that each row, each column and each 3 x 3 frame contains the nine letters from the black box below. The hidden nine-letter word is in the diagonal from top left to bottom right.

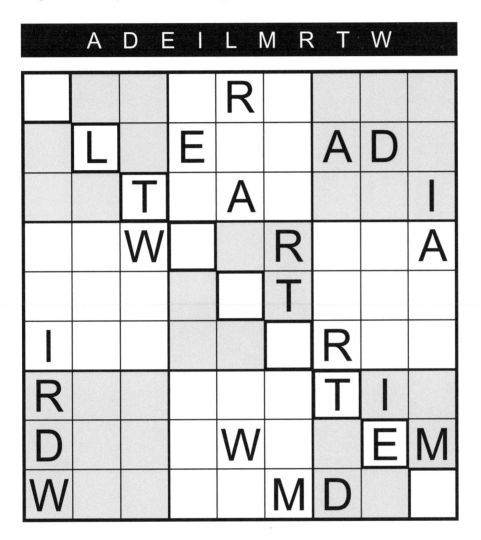

A D E I L M R T W

				R				
	L		E			A	D	
		T		A				I
		W			R			A
					T			
I						R		
R						T		I
D				W			E	M
W					M	D		

DOODLE PUZZLE

A doodle puzzle is a combination of images, letters and/or numbers that represent a word or a concept. If you cannot solve a doodle puzzle, do not look at the answer right away. Think hard—and outside the box.

★★★ BrainSnack®—Outlines

Which letter has the wrong outline color?

UNCANNY TURN

Rearrange the letters of the phrase to form a cognate anagram, one which is related or connected in meaning to the original phrase. The answer can be one or more words.

THE COUGARS

★★★★ **Webster Says Not I** by John M. Samson

ACROSS
1 Sand at Augusta
5 Young herring
10 Caps
14 Suffix with soft or hard
15 Share knowledge
16 Uzbekistan sea
17 Got riled up
18 Zellweger in *Leatherheads*
19 Chest sound
20 War room gathering?
23 Some are rainy
24 Pool temperature tester
25 Trace
26 Corkscrews
31 Tooth type
34 Seabirds
35 By birth
36 Deep blue
37 Found out
38 End of a 12/31 song
39 Antique auto
40 Aches
41 *A Tramp Abroad* author
42 Game in which one knocks
44 "Annabel Lee" poet
45 Id, it's not
46 Penny Marshall TV role
50 Mount Holyoke vis-à-vis Napa Valley College?
55 Film director Kazan
56 Inedible orange
57 Scarlett O'Hara's daughter
58 Smaller amount
59 Speak
60 Pants section
61 Walkway
62 Clairvoyants
63 Newcastle river

DOWN
1 Leafless branches
2 Peep show
3 Sports site
4 Bust site
5 Pearl collection
6 Prepares a banana
7 Bullfrog genus
8 Waldo Pepper et al.
9 Stephen King novel
10 Impaired
11 Quick horse
12 Like John Isner
13 Loom reed
21 Big noise
22 Eternities
26 Like title roles
27 Overthrows first
28 "Storms in Africa" singer

29 "Madonna of the Rosary" artist
30 Visualized
31 Helgenberger of *CSI*
32 "The ___ Love": R.E.M.
33 Penn State mascot
34 Kind of life insurance
37 Funny
38 Most saccharin
40 Quite significant
41 "L'Shana ___" (Rosh Hashanah greeting)
43 Tread old ground
44 Harness horses
46 Olympic sledder
47 Life of ___ (ease)
48 *The Dark Knight* director
49 Related to mom

50 Beatles movie
51 Jejunum neighbors
52 Essential point
53 Renaissance patron
54 See socially

★ Hourglass

Starting in the middle, each word in the top half has the letters of the word below it, plus a new letter, and each word in the bottom half has the letters of the word above it, plus a new letter.

(1) Rodent
(2) Enclosed quarters which are forbidden to men
(3) Dishonor
(4) Similar
(5) Half
(6) Facial expression
(7) Not complicated
(8) Electrical discharge

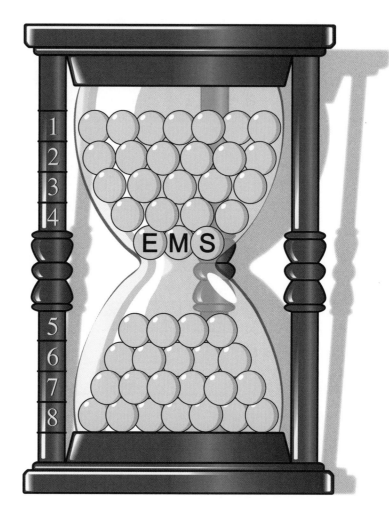

FRIENDS

What do the following words have in common?

DREAM AIR LOVE SEAM TOOTH AGE RELENT

★ Horoscope

Fill in the grid so that every row, every column and every frame of six boxes contains six different symbols: health, work, money, happiness, family and love. Look at the row or column that corresponds with your sign of the zodiac and find out which symbols are important for you today. The symbols appear in increasing order of importance (1–6). It's up to you to interpret the meaning of each symbol to your specific situation.

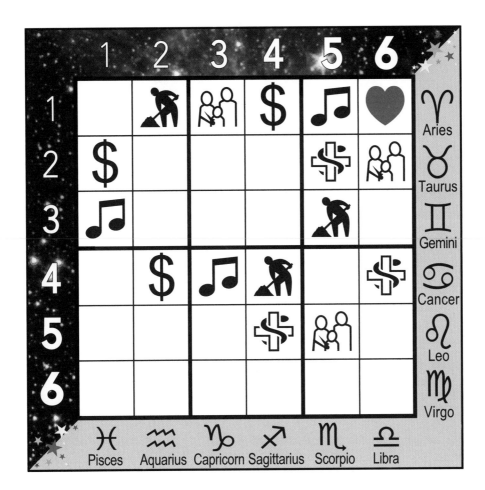

SANDWICH

What four-letter word belongs between the word at left and the word at right, so that the first and second word, and the second and third word, each form a common compound word or phrase?

LEADER _ _ _ _ WRECK

★★★★ Webster Says Not II by John M. Samson

ACROSS

1 Creamy dressing
6 Nonsense poet
10 Talking horse
14 Great Plains hub
15 Knight's wreath
16 "I see," facetiously
17 Animal with a flexible snout
18 Minnesota NHL team
19 Bona fide
20 Remote possibilities?
22 Necessitate
24 Hard to pin down
25 Eldest daughter of Laban
26 Tennis star who wrote *Open*
29 Scold sharply
33 Areas between shoulders?
34 Charlatan
35 Q-Tip
36 Of the ear
37 Eye makeup
38 Boxy transports
39 Bag of chips, say
40 Signs a contract
41 Pig out
42 Super Bowl I winners
44 "Imagine" singer
45 Lewis or Sandburg
46 "The King" of soccer
47 New Englander
50 Japanese dish
54 Third of thrice
55 2011 Kenneth Branagh film
57 Nasal cavity
58 Dog's warning
59 Schlep
60 Like water from a well
61 "A miss ___ good as a mile"
62 Belgian river
63 "___ one" (ticket notation)

DOWN

1 Campus cadet org.
2 *The Joy Luck Club* nanny
3 Mondavi Winery locale
4 Shanghai cloakroom attendants?
5 Trotter's gear
6 Humble
7 Sister of Ares
8 *In toto*
9 Deliverer
10 Stewart's grand cru?
11 Poseidon's mom
12 Morales of *Caprica*
13 Barbie, for one
21 Yalie
23 Catch red-handed
25 Michigan and Ontario
26 Tag ___ with (accompany)
27 Everglades critter
28 Absinthe ingredient
29 Spare and tall
30 NFL Hall-of-Famer Lynn
31 Dance for two
32 *Barnaby Jones* star Buddy
34 Last test
37 Opera text
41 "Summer Rain" singer Carlisle
43 Scots negative
44 Albanian coin
46 Baby food
47 Bear or Berra
48 Sothern and Jillian
49 Hall of Champions org.
50 Barflies
51 Director Avakian
52 Fruit with green pulp
53 "Send in the Clowns" starter
56 ___ polloi

★ Bicycle

All the words are hidden vertically, horizontally or diagonally—in both directions. The letters that remain unused form a sentence from left to right.

```
C Y C L I S R A B E L D N A H
N T G C H A I N B L A D E I S
G E O O D D R U M B R A K E F
O K C O L R T Y O U R H E A L
C C T H P R L E B A S P U M P
A A R A E W N I A R U R A B L
R R E N A W C N R N E K O P S
B B N D H Y S O O I H N T K I
O I H E C E T I C E I T R Y G
N Y E L O C S U A O F O O T N
E L E N E N I D R E F M A E P
S C H L E S L T F R A M E T O
G Y F P E I C O Y N U R F U S
D E S K G P Y E Y B S T E O T
R U A H I E C D N A I T N R I
S R T R O D N F A S T K D E R
B T H A N A C O M P U T E R I
N T H G I L R A E R A C R A R
```

COMPUTER
CYCLISTS
DRUM BRAKE
DYNAMO
FENDER
FORK
FRAME
GEAR
HANDLEBARS
HEADLIGHT
INNER TUBE
LOCK
PEDAL
PUMP
RAINWEAR
REAR LIGHT
REFLECTOR
ROUTE
SIGNPOST
SPOKE
SUSPENSION
WHEELS

BICYCLE   BRAKES   CHAIN BLADE
BRACKET   CARBON   CITY BIKE

LETTERBLOCKS

Move the letterblocks around so that words are formed on top and below that you can associate with herbs and spices.

★★ The Puzzled Librarian

The new library assistant accidentally bumped into the Good Reads notice board, and the magnetic letters all fell off. The librarian remembered the authors' names, but needs some help to get the titles right, as the chief librarian will be back in ten minutes!

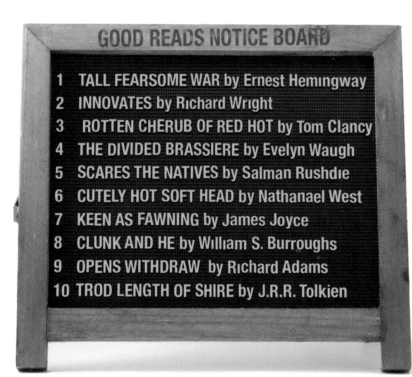

GOOD READS NOTICE BOARD

1   TALL FEARSOME WAR by Ernest Hemingway
2   INNOVATES by Richard Wright
3   ROTTEN CHERUB OF RED HOT by Tom Clancy
4   THE DIVIDED BRASSIERE by Evelyn Waugh
5   SCARES THE NATIVES by Salman Rushdie
6   CUTELY HOT SOFT HEAD by Nathanael West
7   KEEN AS FAWNING by James Joyce
8   CLUNK AND HE by William S. Burroughs
9   OPENS WITHDRAW by Richard Adams
10 TROD LENGTH OF SHIRE by J.R.R. Tolkien

REPOSITION PREPOSITION

Unscramble APRON TUTUS and find a two-word preposition.

★★★★ Themeless by Ralph Small

ACROSS

1 Noah's eldest son
5 Broad necktie
10 Stuffed shirt
14 ___ John's pizza
15 Woody vine
16 Links target
17 One of the 3-R's
19 Singles
20 Paper parts
21 Haulers
23 Birthplace of Ceres
24 "The Colossus" poet
25 Like the Ganges, to Hindus
28 Sentimental object
31 Phoenix nest?
32 Elegant behavior
33 Ad-___ (wing it)
34 Strove (for)
35 Surreptitious looks
36 Autograph hounds
37 Elgar's *Coronation* ___
38 Fleur-___
39 Richard in *The Godfather*
40 Hold back
42 Sable
43 Dr. Hahn of *Grey's Anatomy*
44 Verbal challenge
45 Kind of clause
47 Universal VIP
51 Slovak, e.g.
52 Intimidating
54 Capture
55 Kazakhstan range
56 Chronicle
57 Ampera car company
58 Sudan neighbor
59 Saint Andrews hazard

DOWN

1 Splashy resorts
2 Fox's prey
3 *Paradise Lost* is one
4 Made a difference
5 California nut
6 College near Albany
7 Puma and lynx
8 Pasta suffix
9 Undiplomatic
10 Yells
11 Casual
12 Krupa in *Home Alone 3*
13 Nancy Drew's friend
18 *Tap* star Gregory
22 Emulates Slick Rick
24 High points
25 Relish
26 Cassette front
27 Rich dessert
28 Calvin of fashion
29 *Roots* surname
30 Buddy in *Barnaby Jones*
32 "Salsa Queen" Cruz
35 Tranquil
36 Al Roker's guess
38 Coffee grind
39 Showed concern
41 Vacationer's choice
42 Tomei in *Happy Accidents*
44 How haunted houses are lit
45 Word in Missouri's motto
46 Response to a masher
47 Uninspiring
48 Lift at Taos
49 Korbut the gymnast
50 Swing a sickle
53 Central Florida?

★★★ Sport Maze

Draw the shortest way from the ball to the goal. You can only move along vertical and horizontal lines, not along diagonal lines. The figure on each square indicates the number of squares the ball must be moved in the same direction. You can change direction at each stop.

4	2	4	4	2	3
1	1	4	1	2	●
4	4	1	3	1	4
4	3	1	2	1	5
1	1	4	4	2	2
3	3	5	4	1	4

DOUBLETALK

What word means "departed from" or "remaining"?

★★★ Kakuro

Each number in a black area is the sum of the numbers that you have to enter in the next empty boxes. The empty boxes that make up the sum are called a run. The sum of the across run is written above the diagonal in the black area and the sum of the down run is written below the diagonal. Runs can only contain the numbers 1 through 9 and each number in a run can only be used once. The gray boxes only contain odd numbers and the white only even numbers.

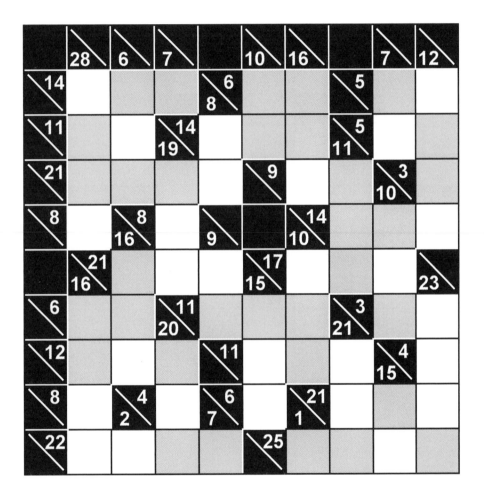

TRANSADDITION

Add one letter to STYLE OF TRIBUTE and rearrange the rest to find a connection.

★★★★ Homophone Humor by Michele Sayer

ACROSS

1 Apple cofounder
5 Eyed impertinently
10 Give up claim to
14 Great Salt Lake state
15 German city near Luxembourg
16 Store sign
17 Illustrator Gustave
18 "I ___ Symphony": Supremes
19 "Cool!"
20 Darling fawn?
22 Outspoken foe of Antony
24 Barefaced
25 Antidote
26 Severe trial
29 Warsaw opinion survey?
33 After-dinner wine
34 Largest Cornhusker city
36 *Star Trek: TNG* counselor
37 *Cold Mountain* heroine
38 Scotch price factor
39 Hip-hop producer Gotti
40 Lower limbs
42 Lott from Mississippi
44 Lit out
45 Chimney sweep uniform?
47 Jack in a nursery rhyme
49 TV's *Deal ___Deal*
50 Danny in *Merry Andrew*
51 Shy pond fish?
54 Canvas clearance?
58 *A Death in the Family* novelist
59 Brief
61 Barbershop job
62 Snitch
63 Nisei's parent
64 Marner's machine
65 Slippery
66 Recompense
67 City in Sicily

DOWN

1 Ashley in *Crossing Over*
2 Sioux speaker
3 Theda in *Cleopatra*
4 Icy dessert
5 Desdemona's love
6 Gordon Gekko's sin
7 Baloney producer?
8 Auction ending
9 Stoker vampire
10 Guiding idea
11 Sword with a bell
12 Pricey
13 Within: Comb. form
21 1988 Meg Ryan film
23 Anger
25 Ben of Ben & Jerry's
26 Pearly gems
27 Clown's workplace
28 *Rocky IV* boxer

29 Debra in *Love Me Tender*
30 Where Betelgeuse is
31 Peter in *Casablanca*
32 Digestive gland
35 Tenor Lanza
41 Black Panther Carmichael
42 Libya neighbor
43 Bangkok cravat?
44 Railroad bridge support
46 "Seats sold out" sign
48 Popeye's love
50 Black or Carpenter
51 Blanchett in *Elizabeth*
52 Double curve
53 Holler
54 Like a .250 batting average

55 *East of Eden* brother
56 Löwenbräu logo
57 *Harry Potter* actress Watson
60 FDR's successor

★★★ BrainSnack®—Missing Corner

Which cube (1–6) fits in the empty corner?

BLOCK ANAGRAM

Form the word that is described in the brackets with the letters above the grid. Extra letters are already in the right place.

TEENAGE (hostile meeting of opposing forces)

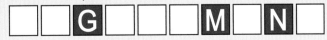

★★★ Word Sudoku

Complete the grid so that each row, each column and each 3 x 3 frame contains the nine letters from the black box below. The hidden nine-letter word is in the diagonal from top left to bottom right.

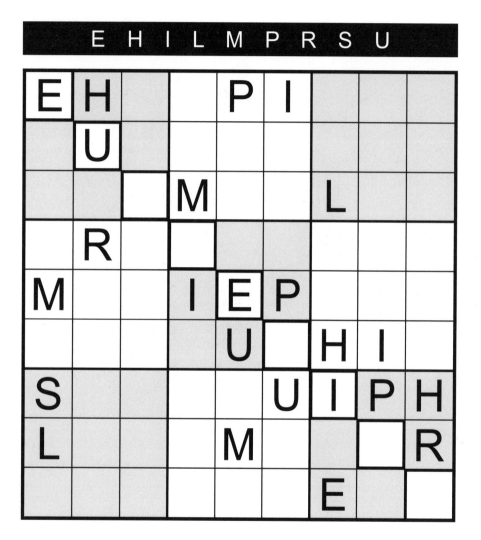

UNCANNY TURN

Rearrange the letters of the phrase to form a cognate anagram, one which is related or connected in meaning.

NO STAMP

★★★ BrainSnack®—Number Block

A number is formed in every group of blocks. Which number (0–5) does not belong?

END GAME

The words you are seeking all have the letters END in them in the position indicated.
When you have found all of the answers, from the clues on the right, one column will reveal the
END GAME word which will give you a space.

_	_	_	_	E	N	D	_	_
			_	_	E	N	D	
E	N	D	_	_	_	_	_	
_	_	_	E	N	D	_	_	

Climbed
A refrain
To make a slave of
One who is present

★★★★ More Homophone Humor by Michele Sayer

ACROSS

1 Semiprecious stone
5 Gas used in lasers
10 Moist
14 Nevada border city
15 Bond actor Roger
16 Lake in HOMES
17 Florentine river
18 MoMA display
19 Playwright Coward
20 Affair of honor for four?
22 Notched a victory, finally
24 McKellen and McEwan
25 Enameled metalware
26 Acclivity
29 Lapin
33 Bridges in *Max Payne*
34 Painter's wear
36 Arizona city
37 Roman houshold god
38 Annoy
39 "Totally cool, man!"
40 Vocalist James
42 Bond girl Roberts
44 Multigenerational tale
45 Tour the Eternal City?
47 Shooting star
49 Andersson in *Persona*
50 About 1.609 kilometers
51 Rival of Athens
54 Slow sales period?
58 Green Hornet's valet
59 Move up socially
61 Opposed
62 Husband of Osiris
63 Seasonal song
64 Clancy hero Jack
65 Be down
66 Like sumo wrestlers
67 Recounted

DOWN

1 Toward the mouth
2 Ecuador neighbor
3 *The King and I* heroine
4 John's place?
5 Totals
6 Rodeo gear
7 World Cup score
8 *Catch-22* pilot
9 1976 Faye Dunaway film
10 Brian in *Cocoon*
11 Suffix for buck
12 Demeanor
13 "O Rei" of soccer
21 Aykroyd in *Ghostbusters*
23 Corrida cheer
25 Tasteless
26 More up to it

27 Defense pact (1954–77)
28 Magna ___
29 Lena in *The Wiz*
30 Mystiques
31 Insect stage
32 Speed tracker
35 Home of the Heat
41 Bierce the cynic
42 Sin-taxed item
43 Friendly
44 Patrick of *X-Men*
46 Henrietta, NY campus
48 Moose relative
50 Notes to employees
51 Read through superficially
52 ___ doble (Spanish dance)
53 Expectant

54 Tightrope
55 War goddess
56 List conclusion
57 Gracious
60 Where Jekyll became Hyde

★★ Sudoku X

Fill in the grid so that each row, each column and each 3 x 3 frame contains every number from 1 to 9. The two main diagonals of the grid also contain every number from 1 to 9.

2		4	1			5		3
	9		2			1	6	8
6			8		5		9	
9	5				8			
	1		7				4	
			9					
						7	5	9
			4		3			
		8						

UNCANNY TURN

Rearrange the letters of the phrase to form a cognate anagram, one which is related or connected in meaning to the original phrase. The answer can be one or more words.

NIGHT WANED

★ Safe Code

To open the safe you have to replace the question marks with the correct figures. You can find these figures by determining the logical methods behind the numbers shown. These methods may include calculation, inversion, repetition, chronological succession, forming ascending and descending series.

SAFE A08

CHANGELINGS

Each of the three lines of letters below spell words which you might have seen at the movies, but the letters have been mixed up. Four letters from the first word are now in the third line, four letters from the third word are in the second line and four letters from the second word are in the first line. The remaining letters are in their original places. What are the words?

G A S A F N A N C R
S O L D T I C G E H
C B A G E C O A L A

★★★★★ What's in a Name I by John M. Samson

ACROSS

1 Singe
5 Polish spots
10 "The rain is ___, the fire Joe ..."
14 Judicial attire
15 No longer anchored
16 ___ Enchanted (2004)
17 Noted cartel
18 "This I ___ see!"
19 Mob scene
20 "Strong-willed warrior" name
22 "Manly" names
24 Small hotel
25 212°F = ___ °C
26 "Broom-covered hill" name
30 "God is my strength" name
34 Chabert in Ghosts of Girlfriends Past
35 Become used to
37 551 on a monument
38 Julius Caesar's love
39 Lessened
40 Soprano Sutherland
41 June bug
42 Books
43 Richard in Ocean's Eleven
44 Nonets
46 Perfumed
48 "Evita" role
49 Three ___ match
50 "Who is like God" name
54 "Gift of God" name
58 1952 Olympics city
59 Letter closing
61 Pail problem
62 Wings
63 Bog bird
64 Not on base
65 Knight and Danson
66 Mr. ___ (2002 Sandler film)
67 "Be" singer Diamond

DOWN

1 It caws for a cause
2 Arizona tribe
3 "Breath" name
4 Easy chair
5 1998 Olympics city
6 Elementary bit
7 NYC subway
8 Ford of the Runaways
9 David Ferrer, for one
10 Overpowering fear
11 "God has helped" name
12 Tortoiselike
13 Junior exams
21 "500" race
23 "___ careful!"
26 Oar part
27 Happy Feet's friend
28 Something to squirrel away
29 Gets warmer?
30 Stab
31 Sarcastic wedding response?
32 Send over the moon
33 Like legal paper
36 Memphis–Chicago dir.
39 Visibly amazed
40 "God has given" name
42 Humorous sound
43 Insulting tip
45 Sonic boomerangs
47 Freewheels
50 Ring around a fort
51 May or Capri
52 Swathed
53 Mezzanine area
54 Early TV equine
55 "Mr. Hockey" Gordie
56 The Time Machine race
57 Oil source
60 Yorkshire river

⋆ Keep Going

Start on a blank square of your choice and connect as many blank squares as possible with one single continuous line. You can only connect squares along vertical and horizontal lines, not along diagonal lines. You must continue the connecting line up until the next obstacle, i.e., the rim of the box, a black square or a square that has already been used. You can change direction at any obstacle you meet. Each square can only be used once. The number of blank squares that will be left unused is marked in the upper square. There is more than one solution. We only show one solution.

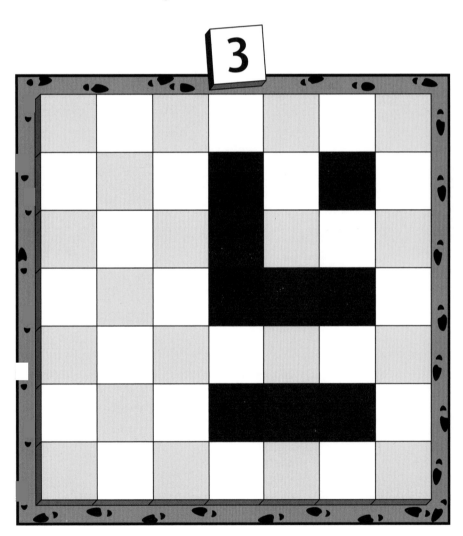

DELETE ONE

Delete one letter from **SMART DIM END** and rearrange the rest to find an appropriate word.

★ Hourglass

Starting in the middle, each word in the top half has the letters of the word below it, plus a new letter, and each word in the bottom half has the letters of the word above it, plus a new letter.

(1) Relating to the central government of a federation
(2) Dreaded
(3) Dimmer
(4) Deprived of the sense of hearing
(5) Struggle
(6) Austrian who originated psychoanalysis
(7) Repay
(8) Beginner

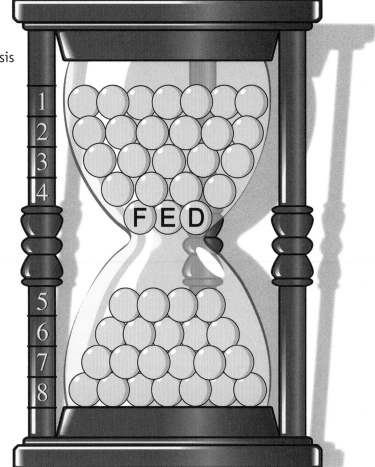

CHANGE ONE

Change one letter in each of these two words to form a common two-word phrase.

ALOUD WINE

★★★★★ What's in a Name II by John M. Samson

ACROSS

1 Offering at VPI
5 Boise's state
10 Ice melter
14 Super's apartment, probably
15 Consumer activist Ralph
16 Storied "gift horse" site
17 Sharif of *Funny Girl*
18 Weary looking
19 Captain, for one
20 "Black" name
22 "Born on Christmas Day" name
24 By means of
25 Cry like a cat
26 "Noble" name
30 "God beholds" name
34 Blackmore heroine
35 Judge Doom's victims
37 Pick, pick, pick
38 Doctrines
39 Social call
40 Medical researcher's goal
41 "Bright" name
42 Italy's fashion capital
43 Prophet in Exodus 7:1
44 Give the once-over
46 Gullywasher
48 Pismire
49 2011 animated film
50 "Son of Matthew" name
54 Floral female name
58 Boom
59 Mr. Philbin
61 Obsessed with
62 German duck
63 *Mr. Palomar* author Calvino
64 Coward of note
65 Numb
66 Lion hero of *Narnia* tales
67 Resort SE of Palermo

DOWN

1 Inn offering
2 "You can't pin this ___!"
3 Greenish blue shade
4 Saharan trains
5 American native
6 Go for it
7 Dental org.: Abbr.
8 Taken down, as a tree
9 Gargoyle, e.g.
10 Peashooters
11 Brackish Asian lake
12 Anderson in *Stroker Ace*
13 Little guy
21 ABBA ballerina
23 Harper in *Tender Mercies*
26 Thin pancakes
27 Bow rub-on
28 "Whole" names
29 Whirling
30 ___ custody
31 Familiarize
32 Leslie in *Gigi*
33 Rep
36 Spanish she-bear
39 "Winner" name
40 "Beautiful woman" name
42 Department with ties
43 Seed case
45 In groups of two
47 Prayer
50 Wilbur's horse
51 Superior rating
52 Information
53 New Jersey cagers
54 "You are mine" name
55 Is hep to
56 Egyptian sun god
57 *Show Boat* girl
60 "Sleepy Time ___"

★★★ BrainSnack®—Recycler

With which recycling logo (A-F) can you make this pattern?

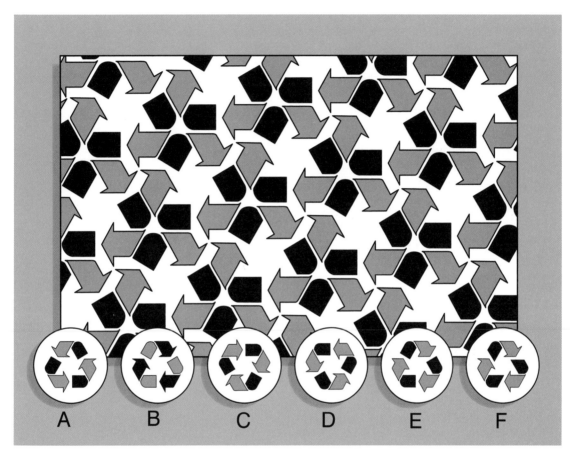

LETTER LINE

Put a letter in each of the squares below to make a word which means "a journey." These numbered clues refer to other words which can be made from the whole.

4 3 10 8 7 SHINE; 5 10 4 8 3 ROYAL; 7 8 9 1 2 10 AN
INDISCRIMINATE COLLECTOR; 6 7 1 10 5 2 3 ENDANGER.

1	2	3	4	5	6	7	8	9	10

★★ Monkey Business

Some of the older students have been monkeying about with the BEST KIDS BOOKS titles list in the library. Can you fix it?

1 PAPER NET
by J.M. BARRIE
2 PUB NATTY HEN
by DOROTHY KUNHARDT
3 PLOT HYPERCARNAL ROUNDHEAD
by CROCKETT JOHNSON
4 GIRLHOOD GLOATING
by PEGGY RATHMAN
5 SAFE NOBLE GANGRENE
by L.M. MONTGOMERY

ONE LETTER LESS OR MORE

The word on the right side contains the letters of the word on the left side plus or minus the letter in the middle. One letter is already in the right place.

| L | I | N | G | E | R | I | E | +V | | | L | | | | | | |

★★★★★ Groaners by Tim Wagner

ACROSS

1 Pinch of salt
5 Mountain nymph
10 Not illusory
14 Lacoste founder Lacoste
15 1996 Olympic gymnast Strug
16 Spicy stew
17 Pitching stats
18 Bright star in Virgo
19 British spa
20 Finger counter?
23 Inevitability
24 Surgery sites, briefly
25 Org. with a journal
26 Ottawa hockey team
31 *I Can't Sleep* playwright
34 ___ longlegs
35 Cannabis
36 Fountain of jazz
37 Judi Dench et al.
38 Lugosi in *Mark of the Vampire*
39 *Baudolino* novelist
40 Pal of Pythias
41 Monster Muppet
42 Pronounces guilty
44 It makes "adverb" an adjective
45 Thurman in *Gattaca*
46 Crude
50 Nosy simian?
55 Kosovo native
56 *As You Like It* lady
57 Irving's world authority
58 Pierre's brainstorm
59 Suffix with fraud
60 Latin 101 verb
61 Realtor's sign
62 Broadway boards
63 Ownership paper

DOWN

1 Judicial Stallone role
2 Osprey nest
3 Bumps in the road
4 Look before you leap
5 Gold medalist Baiul
6 Response
7 Schmidt of Google
8 Sacramento Kings arena
9 Red suit
10 Brawny
11 Israeli resort
12 Der ___ (Adenauer)
13 Lionized actor?
21 Robbins and Rice
22 Recite the rosary
26 Island where Aesop lived
27 Early garden
28 German auto pioneer
29 Croissant
30 Legal delay
31 Crude bunch?
32 Art ___
33 Stiff collar
34 Rhett Butler's final word
37 Middle East capital
38 Was a member
40 Showroom model
41 Tostada relative
43 Nicknamed
44 One with convictions
46 Doing something with
47 Tsarist decree
48 Of few words
49 Overpromoted
50 Electric flux symbols
51 Makeover
52 Turgenev's birth city
53 Druid, for example
54 Endoscopy focuses

★★★ Sport Maze

Draw the shortest way from the ball to the goal. You can only move along vertical and horizontal lines, not along diagonal lines. The figure on each square indicates the number of squares the ball must be moved in the same direction. You can change direction at each stop.

5	5	5	1	1	5
2	1	3	4	2	1
4	2	1	0	2	4
1	3	1	1	2	3
4	1	4	2	3	2
1	1	5		2	3

UNCANNY TURN

Rearrange the letters of the phrase to form a cognate anagram, one which is related or connected in meaning to the original phrase. The answer can be one or more words.

OH FINE DRESS GAIN

★★★ Word Sudoku

Complete the grid so that each row, each column and each 3 x 3 frame contains the nine letters from the black box below. The hidden nine-letter word is in the diagonal from top left to bottom right.

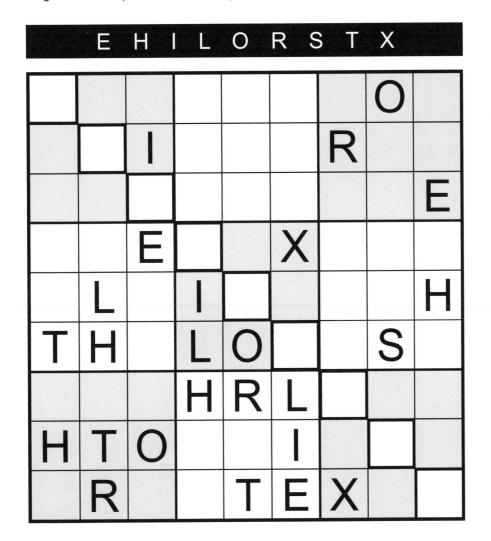

E H I L O R S T X

DOODLE PUZZLE

A doodle puzzle is a combination of images, letters and/or numbers that represent a word or a concept. If you cannot solve a doodle puzzle, do not look at the answer right away. Think hard—and outside the box.

FAST

★ Spot the Differences

Find the nine differences in the image on the right.

DELETE ONE

Delete one letter from CAPITAL MANGO CHECKS and shake up the rest to mix a classic drink.

★★★★★ More Groaners by Tim Wagner

ACROSS

1 Sonic boomers of yore
5 Floral feature
10 Take a catnap
14 Word form for "high"
15 Noted violin maker
16 Aunt Bee's grandnephew
17 Frost product
18 Calligraphy stroke
19 Diamond of the underworld
20 Debugging aid?
23 Totally trash
24 ___ Lung in *Kung Fu Panda*
25 Suffix for bombard
26 Eyelet creator
31 Old-fashioned pen
34 Utter bore
35 Chewie's copilot
36 Skye in *Moonglow*
37 Angelic glows
38 Garr in *Tootsie*
39 Ornamental pond fish
40 Direction indicator
41 Niacin source
42 Was really offensive?
44 MapQuest's owner
45 Gun lobbyists' org.
46 Formula math
50 Dupe being taken for a ride?
55 Cabbage salad
56 Alaska's first capital
57 Sitarist Shankar
58 Hercules' captive
59 Prank
60 Work without ___ (be daring)
61 Headliner
62 Steamy place
63 ___ *Breckinridge*

DOWN

1 Mouth-watering
2 Biscuit's kin
3 Long lock
4 Occasional
5 Flock's overseer
6 Abrasive mineral
7 Lentil-like weed
8 Expectant
9 Mortal span
10 Hall-of-Famer Fingers
11 Fencer's foil
12 Autograph
13 Trial balloon
21 Manitoba native
22 *Fiesque* composer
26 Chowder fish
27 Freeze follower
28 "Take ___ Train"
29 Seadogs
30 "Don't count ___ !"

31 Rock rabbit
32 Fenced goods
33 Part of ICU
34 "You bet!"
37 Hope is found there
38 Ancestor of a text message
40 Ranch unit
41 Boo-Boo's buddy
43 *Jeopardy!* question
44 Peruvian wool
46 *Chicago Hope* star
47 Cecil's cartoon pal
48 Pirate ship
49 Baker of soul music
50 Pitchfork-shaped letters
51 Quite frequently
52 Hacienda room
53 Gershon in *Showgirls*
54 Caesarian delivery?

★★ Sudoku X

Fill in the grid so that each row, each column and each 3 x 3 frame contains every number from 1 to 9. The two main diagonals of the grid also contain every number from 1 to 9.

		7						
	9		3	5				
							9	6
		5			9		3	
					1		5	
	4					7	2	9
				3		4		
				9	4		1	
4	8		1		6			

FRIENDS

What do the following words have in common?

BIOGRAPHY GRAPH MATES PILOT SUGGEST

★ Social Contact

All the words are hidden vertically, horizontally or diagonally—in both directions. The letters that remain unused form a sentence from left to right.

```
B Y B D O O F L N P A T U R M
Y L O O H C S E O H U D U U M
R A N B J H E I N V A O S G S
A S H O P I A S D N E I R F C
R E G A L L I V C R C E I G O
B N E C P D R E H T E G O T F
I H C F A R L I N C E D T O F
L O I A R E L I V O E G W E E
I B F M T N E V E L Y N V T E
H B F I N H S E N L S I I L T
H Y O L E G I A E E E D V I H
I O T Y R U H N C C Y D F S C
O R S T H A O T E T E E N T U
E P O P U L A R R E I W D E O
S O F M I E M A B I E V R N T
N O I T A T I V N I B S I O F
V I S I T N A T H M E E T T E
I R S G I F T L O C I E T Y Y
```

EVENT	MUSIC	
FAMILY	OFFICE	
FOOD	PARTNER	
FRIENDS	POPULAR	
GIFT	RECEIVE	
GROUP	SCHOOL	
HOBBY	SHOP	
HOSPITAL	TOGETHER	
INVITATION	TOUCH	
JOB	TRAIN	
LAUGH	VILLAGE	
LIBRARY	VISIT	
LISTEN	WEDDING	
LONELY		
LOVE		
MEET		

ACTIVITY	CHILDREN	COLLECT
BIRTH	COFFEE	DANCE

SANDWICH

What five-letter word belongs between the word at left and the word at right, so that the first and second word, and the second and third word, each form a common compound word or phrase?

B O D Y _ _ _ _ _ R A I L

★★★★★ Themeless by Ralph Small

ACROSS

1 Feline weapon
5 Small Old World lizard
10 RBI, for one
14 Swiss Rhine feeder
15 Having legal force
16 Moon over Paris
17 Italian ham
19 Works in the Prado
20 Capital of Chile
21 Sex Pistols frontman
23 Suffix for disk
24 Biblical ziggurat
25 Court ruling
28 Hired hands
31 *The Horse Whisperer* novelist
32 Place for a bride and her father
33 Ad catchword
34 Head lice
35 2004 Jude Law film
36 "Ask ___ questions ..."
37 Summer, in Paris
38 Stigmas
39 One making a pit stop
40 Scottish instruments
42 Like the Witch of the West
43 Vows
44 Army level
45 Lasik target
47 "Tommyrot!"
51 Lena in *The Ninth Gate*
52 Loud
54 S or M, e.g.
55 U.S. Open winner Els
56 Irradiate
57 Angled a nail
58 In a tough spot
59 A consort of Zeus

DOWN

1 Puts a limit on
2 Flynn Boyle of films
3 *127 Hours* subject Ralston
4 Wayne's world?
5 Handle a joystick
6 Gun barrel measurement
7 Vocal range
8 Buzz Aldrin's alma mater
9 Cherubic
10 Christian in *Bobby*
11 Sweater style
12 Put in one's chips
13 Youngest voter
18 Gives a ticket to
22 Double-reed woodwind
24 Fundamental ingredient
25 Star in the Swan
26 Musical set in Argentina
27 Group *Jeopardy!* answers
28 London elevators
29 Zellweger in *Miss Potter*
30 Cold steel
32 Lily relatives
35 Kind of soup
36 Herring eater
38 Take the bait
39 Washer cycle
41 Given a one-star review
42 Word on a poster
44 Riveter of the 1940s
45 Buyer's concern
46 Eclectic mix
47 Prime-time hour
48 1899 gold rush site
49 Interview attire
50 Idaho motto starter
53 Bruin teammate of Espo

★★★ BrainSnack®—Getting Shirty

Which polo shirt (1-5) doesn't belong in this series?

LETTERBLOCKS

Move the letterblocks around so that words are formed on top and below that you can associate with the environment.

★ Tennis Players

All the words are hidden vertically, horizontally or diagonally—in both directions. The letters that remain unused form a sentence from left to right.

```
S A R P M A S T O I D U A G E
T N N U I U S O R I G I N A G
E T E D S I S K I E F E R N N
P G I L B E R T E N G L A A G
A G A S S I D N E D A H S N R
N S D H A S B S L R C I E E E
E E H N P L A C K E T Y T O B
K E D E I N O I T I N F S R D
N A L B A N D I A N A D C N E
B V O N N L T L E R M P L E O
E R E O A A U P O R T A S C R
C Y R D F R O R B L A K E M M
K S A H E W I T T E S C A S H
E N K G I V N C E C T H E E N
R I O S D O D F T O G H E N I
N K R A J I C E K N E R T E E
R E D N A L I W M T N T O H C
E N A T F E D E R E R U R B Y
```

FEDERER
GAUDIO
GERULAITIS
GILBERT
HEWITT
KIEFER
KORDA
KRAJICEK
LECONTE
LENDL
MCENROE
MEDVEDEV
MUSTER
NADAL
NALBANDIAN
PORTAS
RAFTER
RIOS
RUSEDSKI
SAMPRAS
STEPANEK
WILANDER

AGASSI
ASHE
BECKER

BLAKE
BORG
CASH

CHANG
CONNORS
EDBERG

CHANGE ONE

Change one letter in each of these two words to form a common two-word phrase.

BLUSH FIND

★★★★★ 9-Letter Isograms by John M. Samson

ACROSS

1 Seductive spy Hari
5 Sinbad, for one
9 Man-made waterway
14 Islamic spiritual leader
15 NASCAR legend Yarborough
16 Mad Hatter's guest
17 Basking layabout
19 Constitutional guarantee
20 Some Alaska natives
21 Commits arson
23 One at ease
24 ___-yourself kit
25 Word before many words
27 Daily pill
30 Ration
33 Utensils
35 100 square meters
36 Part of speech
37 Singer Osmond
38 Newsman Hume
39 Mom's specialty
40 Column style
41 "God ___ us ...": Tiny Tim
42 Previously
44 Birthright seller in Genesis
46 *Rosamund* composer
47 Concise summary
51 Finer points
54 Hand bomb
55 Sambuca flavoring
56 Nom de plume
58 Neighborhood eyesore
59 Oily acronym
60 Songs for one
61 Iditarod racers
62 Gate
63 Slithery swimmers

DOWN

1 Fagin, for one
2 Get a grin out of
3 Combat vehicles
4 Drive to achieve
5 SAG in the middle
6 Sounds from fans
7 Partner of cakes
8 Ernie's pal
9 Inducements
10 Silverstone in *Batman & Robin*
11 Bad dream
12 Need an ice bag, e.g.
13 "___ go!"
18 Catkin
22 *Swan Lake* swan
26 Fur seal
27 Diva's "instrument"
28 Perfume source
29 New Jersey cagers
30 Square column
31 Laze on deck
32 Highly profitable
34 "Either he goes ___ go!"
37 Heidi Klum, for one
38 Prude
40 Charlie ___ Band
41 Stripped
43 Removed
45 "Blue" evergreen
48 Adirondack craft
49 Tennyson poem, e.g.
50 Final Four games
51 Morse code clicks
52 Organic compound
53 Cup of tea
54 Carnival freak
57 Boston-area deli

★ Sudoku Twin

Fill in the grid so that each row, each column and each 3 x 3 frame contains every number from 1 to 9. A sudoku twin is two connected 9 x 9 sudokus.

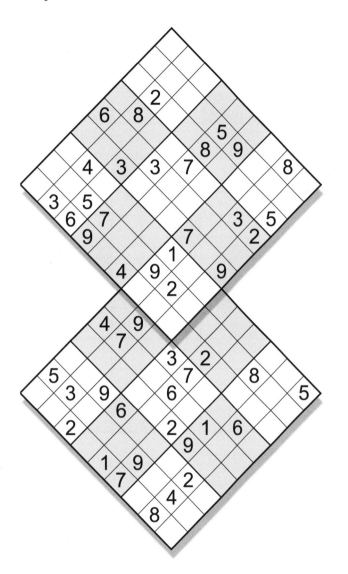

REPOSITION PREPOSITION

Unscramble DIE OF SIN and find a two-word preposition.

★★ Keep Going

Start on a blank square of your choice and connect as many blank squares as possible with one single continuous line. You can only connect squares along vertical and horizontal lines, not along diagonal lines. You must continue the connecting line up until the next obstacle, i.e., the rim of the box, a black square or a square that has already been used. You can change direction at any obstacle you meet. Each square can only be used once. The number of blank squares that will be left unused is marked in the upper square. There is more than one solution. We only show one solution.

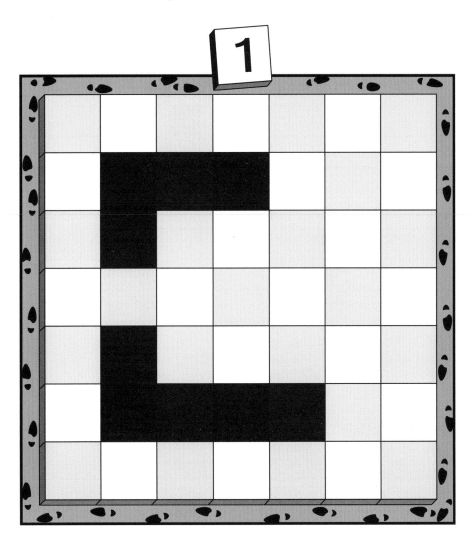

DOUBLETALK

What word means "to withstand" or "to wear away"?

★★★★★ 10-Letter Isograms by John M. Samson

ACROSS

1 Auction bids
5 Spiky-horned antelope
10 Floored it
14 Charles Lamb
15 Its symbol is Rn
16 ___ doble (bullfight music)
17 Rule
19 Prefix for sphere
20 Makes secure
21 Scrounge
23 Something to poach
24 Gordon Ramsay, for one
25 Cereal toppers
29 Hang tough
32 "___ we a pair?"
33 Clan chief of old Scotland
35 E-5, for one
36 Scruff of the neck
37 Place for a basket
38 Purim month
39 Tempe college
40 Specie
41 Silvery fish
42 Matt of *Episodes*
44 Anthony in *Zodiac*
46 Rents out
47 Cash extension?
48 Foreboding
51 Apprentice
55 Puerto ___
56 Native country
58 Winglike
59 Moral
60 Big cat
61 Diane in *Secretariat*
62 Perch in a coop
63 Mexican pot

DOWN

1 Squishy ball
2 Olive in a Caesar salad?
3 Excavates
4 Dessert wine
5 House of William III
6 Hamelin problem
7 "Big Daddy" Amin
8 Upside of a recession
9 Guileless
10 Places to park
11 Trailblazer
12 Cullen family matriarch
13 Portal
18 Licit
22 German river
25 Trite
26 Remove from memory
27 House party?

28 Like Spock
29 Examine grammatically
30 Sterilize by boiling
31 Law school class
34 Savage
37 Many a pollee
38 Texas city
40 "The Censor" of Rome
41 Take an oath
43 "The Raven" maiden
45 Person-to-person
48 Viva voce
49 Kunis in *Black Swan*
50 "And ___ bed": Pepys
51 What we have here
52 Execute perfectly
53 Hydroxyl compund
54 Dame Everage
57 Nobelist Le Duc ___

★ Monkey Business

Some of the older students have been monkeying about with the BEST KIDS BOOKS titles list in the library. Can you fix it?

1 EGOS UP ETHYL ALCOHOL
by DR. SEUSS
2 I SCOURGE ROGUE
by H.A. REY
3 THE THINKING ETHNIC
by MAURICE SENDAK
4 AMEN IDLE
by LUDWIG BEMELMANS
5 HOW DO YOU DO SADIST
OR GNASHING
by JANE YOLEN

CHANGE ONE

Change one letter in each of these two words to form a common two-word phrase.

LOOSE BURPS

★ Public Transportation

All the words are hidden vertically, horizontally or diagonally—in both directions. The letters that remain unused form a sentence from left to right.

```
A N I A R T D E E P S H G I H
C O M P A N Y R I K L C K S H
A W A R T K O I N D I A O F B
I C F R O Y Y I C L E R C T A
T X A I R T A A T N D A T O M
I M R O E R C W U A N T A S L
M B E L G E E U L E T A N H I
E P D M N V Y G D I A S C L C
T A O N E I B T I N A A E C C
A O D T S R N S I O O R I D O
B N G E S D J R E C N C D A N
L S I A A S F U E O R A R M N
E F N G P U U G N Y O E L F E
P A G U H B A B B C A L T I C
T R A I N T I C K E T L C N T
L E U F S T B R A N S I E P I
L A P I C I N U M O R T O D O
A T I O T R A N S F E R N N N
```

PASSENGER
RAILWAY
REGIONAL
STAGE-COACH
STATION
STRIKE
TIMETABLE
TRAIN TICKET
TRAM
TRANSFER

BUS DRIVER	DELAY	INTERCITY
BUS STOP	FARE	JUNCTION
COMPANY	FARE-DODGING	LOCAL
CONDUCTOR	FUEL	MUNICIPAL
CONNECTION	HIGH-SPEED TRAIN	NIGHT BUS

TRANSADDITION

Add one letter to HI RATTLE AND ROAR and rearrange the rest to find a connection.

★★★★★ Double Entendres I by John M. Samson

ACROSS

1 Pedestal part
5 UK political party
10 Suffix with hip or tip
14 Grand saga
15 Troop campsite
16 Made the event
17 Judge's seat
18 *Love Story* author
19 This and that
20 Poachers, e.g.?
23 Hawaiian staple
24 Ho ___ Minh City
25 Olympic swimmer Pablo
29 Otologist's concern
33 "When You Wish ___ Star"
34 Sample
36 Rhone tributary
37 RN's imperative
38 Burn a joss stick
39 Locate
40 Twitch
41 *The Vampire Diaries* heroine
42 Valley ___, PA
43 Honors student
45 Had desires
47 "___ a pity"
48 Paris–Amsterdam dir.
49 Twenty in the brass section, e.g.?
58 Prefix for gram
59 Man of Qum
60 Celebes ox
61 Eye drop?
62 Available money
63 Czech, e.g.
64 Tote-board numbers
65 It'll help you raise dough
66 Newcastle river

DOWN

1 Visa balance
2 On ___ with (equal)
3 Pet of Fred and Wilma
4 Junk mail addressee, often
5 Nielsen in *Spy Hard*
6 To ___ (exactly)
7 Sacks
8 Sushi fish
9 Move
10 Nova ___
11 Narrative
12 Arab potentate
13 Model T contemporaries
21 Gaucho weapon
22 German-Czech river
25 Essentials
26 Ocular nerve

27 Terminix target
28 Longhorn
29 Montaigne piece
30 Scottish terrier
31 Door hanger
32 Finalized
35 Vickers of fiction
38 Protect sensitive information
39 Weatherman's guess
41 Fashion designer Saab
42 Audience
44 Not you and me
46 Join
49 *Beetle Bailey* bulldog
50 Clarinet insert
51 Robed
52 Not distorted
53 Frog genus
54 No ifs, ___ ...

55 None other but
56 Horse of a certain color
57 Overhang

★★ Sunny Weather

Where will the sun shine? With the knowledge that each arrow points to a place where a symbol should be, can you locate the sunny spots? The symbols cannot be next to each other vertically, horizontally or diagonally. A symbol cannot be placed on top of an arrow. We show one symbol.

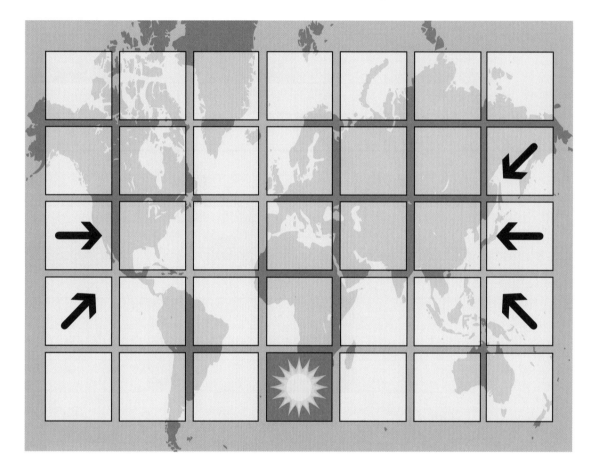

BLOCK ANAGRAM

Form the words that are described in the brackets with the letters above the grid. Extra letters are already in the right place.

PROTESTER (police officer)

★★★ BrainSnack®—Pricey Paint

Each spray can has three symbols indicating the price. According to the table of comparison, which spray can (1–5) is the most expensive?

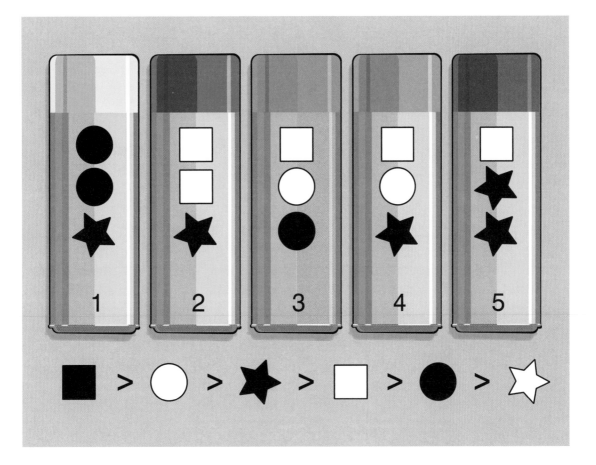

END GAME

The words you are seeking all have the letters END in them in the position indicated. When you have found all of the answers, from the clues on the right, one column will reveal the END GAME word which will give you something to navigate around.

_ E N D _ _ _ _	Capable of being torn
E N D _ _ _ _ _	Living within an animal as a parasite
E N D _ _ _ _ _	Nativeness
_ _ _ E N D _ _	Added to a social networking list

★★★★★ Double Entendres II by John M. Samson

ACROSS

1 Speak with a thick tongue
5 "I ___ Symphony": Supremes
10 ___ Bator, Mongolia
14 One of the Aleutians
15 Archer's need
16 Forbiddance
17 Read a barcode
18 "The Painted" vessel of 1492
19 Geraint's wife
20 Nightcaps for Munchkins?
23 Get the picture
24 Sister of Helios
25 Money of Kabul
29 Everlasting
33 Cause of black ice
34 Ladies' man
36 Palme ___ (Cannes award)
37 Wood stack
38 Freezing
39 Rottweiler in *Up*
40 Supply with guns
41 Fiorentino in *Men in Black*
42 Willis Tower, formerly
43 Sea voyage
45 Kitchen whistlers
47 "Is it a boy ___ girl?"
48 Rent
49 Anemometers, e.g.?
58 Parka part
59 Removed a wreck
60 *Hurlyburly* playwright
61 Great Plains tribe
62 Ready to explode
63 Etc. relative
64 "Red Vines" singer Aimee
65 Inspected the joint
66 Nickelodeon explorer

DOWN

1 Highland girl
2 Sumac symptom
3 Asterisk
4 Castigated
5 Befall
6 Little Mermaid's love
7 Florentine river
8 Campus cadet org.
9 Left Slumberland
10 Apprehensive
11 Anderson in *The Jayne Mansfield Story*
12 Indigo plant
13 Auction bids
21 Carnivore craving
22 Hustle and bustle
25 Opus Award org.
26 Flower goddess
27 Bacteria
28 Peace goddess
29 Boat used in Alaska
30 Deserving a ten
31 ___ Dame
32 Fenway Park surface
35 Like Methuselah
38 Whopping
39 One-upped
41 "Take Me" singer White
42 Spoon handle
44 Soaked
46 Avoided capture
49 "Of ___ are you speaking?"
50 Scintilla
51 Lunch hour
52 Short-billed rail
53 "___ the night before ..."
54 Neutral network
55 Military alliance
56 Ski conveyance
57 Israeli tennis player Dudi

★★ The Puzzled Librarian

The new library assistant accidentally bumped into the Good Reads notice board, and the magnetic letters all fell off. The librarian remembered the authors' names, but needs some help to get the titles right, as the chief librarian will be back in ten minutes!

GOOD READS NOTICE BOARD

1 LARGE ALTHOUGH ACE PIG by Alexander Solzhenitsyn

2 SHOCKERS MADE FOR THE NOVEL SLEUTH by A. Conan Doyle

3 HOT TALE ENDS HEAD MAN by Ernest Hemingway

4 CHIEF THAT LOST NO SHAME by James Fenimore Cooper

5 ASTERN RUDE SAIL by Robert Louis Stevenson

6 THE TASTY BEGGAR by F. Scott Fitzgerald

7 STREAKS ON AND ON by Arthur Koestler

8 IT WOKE ALLIANCE by Nevil Shute

9 DEFT HOGS THIEVE NOW by Henry James

10 SOFT LETHAL MENACE by Dashiell Hammett

MISSING LETTER PROVERB

Fill in each missing letter, indicated by an X, to make a well-known proverb.

LOVX XXXX XXXX X XXX

★ Shipping

All the words are hidden vertically, horizontally or diagonally—in both directions. The letters that remain unused form a sentence from left to right.

```
A S U E Z C A N A L B I T L E
S S T R E N I A T N O C H K P
A N S N F R I G A T E I C I N
T E T A R O H C N A Y O H P E
P R O V I S I O N S L S A I L
R H O R E L L E P O R P F C E
N I Y P R T O O F A I N E R E
C N A N T E E R W R D I R E S
A E W N A M P C T R I A R K U
R B R O A N A E A A L T Y N O
G A E S W N E O E O R P L A H
O R T D O G B P D W T A R T T
S G A E D R I A D E S C E S H
H E W E A L O C C U P E R A G
I S R T O V I A S H I R N G I
P D S T R E K N A T L I O I L
P P P A N A M A C A N A L T M
I N G L A N D I N G C R A F T
```

PANAMA CANAL
PILOT
PORT
PROPELLER
PROVISIONS
RHINE BARGE
SAIL
SAILOR
STARBOARD
SUEZ CANAL
TORPEDO
WARSHIP
WATERWAY

ANCHOR
CANOE
CAPTAIN
CARGO SHIP
CONTAINER

DREDGE
FERRY
FRIGATE
GAS TANKER
LANDING CRAFT

LIGHTHOUSE
LOCK
MAST
MINESWEEPER
OIL TANKER

DELETE ONE

Delete one letter from ICE BEER NEXT GYM and rearrange the rest to find a quick way out.

★ Mammals

All the words are hidden vertically, horizontally or diagonally—in both directions. The letters that remain unused form a sentence from left to right.

```
T H B U M B A B O O N A N W G
N B I E I N G S W C H I M O I
A A S G O A T O B R L P A C R
H N O X D R O M E D A R Y A A
P E N N E D Z E A E K E S M F
E Y A G M S D N V G C D D E F
L H I O G I R B E O A O R L E
E T U B O N S O R R J L E A L
L S E O K A P I H I B P I E L
E F L R A B B I T L O H N O H
N L A R A U G A J L T I D G A
G O H E G D E H E A T N E Z M
H W W O M B A T T O E T E Y S
A O O R A G N A K H R B R E T
R E H T N A P E A N R T A K E
E S Q U I R R E L A H L R N R
O P O I D F R A E B R A L O P
A M I L P O R C U P I N E D Y
```

DROMEDARY
ELEPHANT
GIRAFFE
GOAT
GORILLA
HAMSTER
HARE
HEDGEHOG
HORSE
HYENA
JACKAL
JAGUAR
KANGAROO
LYNX
OKAPI
OTTER
PANTHER
POLAR BEAR
PORCUPINE
RABBIT
REINDEER
SEAL
SQUIRREL
TIGER
WHALE
WOLF
WOMBAT
WOOD MOUSE
ZEBRA

ANTELOPE   BISON   DEER
BABOON   CAMEL   DOLPHIN
BEAVER   COW   DONKEY

MISSING LETTER PROVERB

Fill in each missing letter, indicated by an X, to make a well-known proverb.

XNE XOLXNXEER IX XORTX XEN XXESSED XEN

★ Word Pyramid

Each word in the pyramid has the letters of the word above it, plus a new letter.

I

(1) Iowa
(2) Independent agency of the United States government
(3) Andean civilization
(4) Frenzied
(5) Professional killer
(6) Mechanical device
(7) Presidents

LETTER LINE

Put a letter in each of the squares below to make a word which means "uprising." These numbered clues refer to other words which can be made from the whole.

3 8 9 5 2 10 7 WITH FORCE; 3 8 1 7 6 2 MORAL EXCELLENCE; 6 10 3 2 8 5 REVEAL; 10 9 3 2 5 INTERESTINGLY UNUSUAL.

1	2	3	4	5	6	7	8	9	10

★ Spot the Differences

Find the nine differences in the image on the right.

DELETE ONE

Delete one letter from ANAGRAM RIND STONE and rearrange the rest to find something delicious.

★★★★★ To the Letter by Peggy O'Shea

ACROSS

1 Trough fare
5 Muffler
10 Poverty, metaphorically
14 Musical epilogue
15 "The Last Supper" is one
16 Put-in-Bay's lake
17 Korolev or Stravinsky
18 Beneficial
19 Hitching ___
20 M
23 Dr. Scholl's product
24 LaSalle or DeSoto
25 Morse code T's
27 Specified
31 ___ Lanka
34 "Roger, ___"
36 Cuddly Muppet
37 OA
41 Western tribe
42 Tony contender
43 Pupil's place
44 Spanish Armada ship
47 Med. school course
49 Tiny one
50 Useless
54 NS
60 Present opening
61 Room with hot rocks
62 "Be that ___ may ..."
63 Melville book
64 Human foible
65 Disneyland attraction
66 Burg
67 Worrisome Muppet
68 Certain plaintiff, at law

DOWN

1 Bradbury's bailiwick
2 Start an email session
3 What baking soda neutralizes
4 Analyzed grammatically
5 Fruity concoction
6 Link site
7 In ___ (stuck)
8 Hasty
9 Take for a sucker
10 Scoop seeker
11 Schoenberg's *Moses und* ___
12 Nub
13 Genesis sibling
21 Dragged fishing net
22 Efface
26 *Doonesbury* reverend
27 Terra ___ pottery
28 Popular plant gel
29 "Wherever ___ Roam": Metallica
30 Bump on a log
31 Urban pall
32 Poet laureate Dove
33 Matinee ___
35 Ozone pollutant: Abbr.
38 Erasure
39 Like some degrees
40 Sister of Polyhymnia
45 "Do Ya" rock group
46 Counteracted
48 New Zealand port
51 Saharan spring
52 Nasty and insinuating
53 Cosmetics name
54 Booty
55 Need for heat
56 It can cover a lot of ground
57 Empty container weight
58 Work from a mound
59 Tautomeric compound

PAGE 15

Fruit Punch

S	P	I	T		D	O	L	T	S		R	O	M	P
A	I	D	A		I	N	U	R	E		E	R	I	E
N	E	E	D		F	E	L	O	N		P	A	L	E
G	R	A	P	E	F	R	U	I	T		A	N	O	N
			O	D	E	S			I	D	I	G		
A	M	B	L	E	R		H	U	N	D	R	E	D	S
V	A	L	E	N		B	O	N	E	S		B	I	P
A	N	A	S		S	E	P	A	L		C	O	C	O
I	I	C		A	C	R	E	S		H	O	W	T	O
L	A	K	E	L	A	N	D		C	O	L	L	A	R
		B	A	E	R			C	O	L	D			
A	L	E	G		C	H	E	R	R	Y	P	I	C	K
G	I	R	L		E	A	G	E	R		L	O	R	I
E	T	R	E		L	L	A	M	A		A	W	O	L
D	A	Y	S		Y	O	D	E	L		Y	A	W	N

PAGE 16

Number Cluster

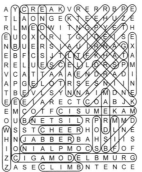

ONE LETTER LESS OR MORE

PIANIST

PAGE 17

BrainSnack®—Jump to It

69. Add 1 to the previous number, reverse the digits and add 1 more.

UNCANNY TURN

IS ABC

PAGE 18

ABBA Hits

M	I	L	L		S	C	O	R	E		C	H	U	M
E	L	I	A		T	A	L	O	N		O	O	N	A
O	I	N	K		E	R	I	K	A		S	N	I	T
W	A	T	E	R	L	O	O		M	O	T	E	T	S
		L	U	L	L		T	O	D	A	Y			
H	A	V	A	N	A		H	A	R	D	S	H	I	P
O	Z	O	N	E		D	O	M	E	S		O	N	E
S	T	U	D		B	I	P	E	D		A	N	T	E
N	E	L		L	I	N	E	R		K	N	E	E	L
I	C	E	B	E	R	G	S		S	A	T	Y	R	S
		Z	E	S	T	Y		A	C	H	E			
L	A	V	I	S	H		F	E	R	N	A	N	D	O
E	B	O	N		D	O	U	S	E		T	E	R	N
S	L	U	G		A	R	R	O	W		E	R	I	C
T	E	S	S		Y	E	L	P	S		R	O	P	E

PAGE 19

Verbs

A verb, together with its subject and possibly a direct object, forms the basis of a sentence.

CHANGE ONE

DROP OUT

PAGE 20

Keep Going

FRIENDS

Each can have the prefix SUPER- to form a new word.

PAGE 21

Popular Pets

C	O	M	P		S	T	O	P	S		L	A	M	A
A	M	A	R		E	A	D	I	E		I	G	O	R
S	A	T	O		S	P	I	C	A		C	R	O	P
T	H	E	C	A	T	I	N	T	H	E	H	A	T	
E	A	R	L	I	E	R		O	W	E				
			A	N	T		S	E	R	E	N	A	D	E
O	R	B	I	T		C	L	A	S	S		R	A	T
L	O	A	M		C	E	A	S	E		S	I	L	O
A	A	R		S	A	D	I	E		S	W	A	I	N
F	R	I	G	H	T	E	N		B	E	I			
			H	A	H		G	R	A	N	D	E	E	
	A	D	O	G	O	F	F	L	A	N	D	E	R	S
E	R	O	S		L	I	L	A	C		L	E	N	T
D	A	R	T		I	S	E	R	E		E	R	S	E
E	L	K	S		C	H	E	E	R		R	E	T	E

PAGE 22

Sudoku

3	1	5	8	6	9	7	4	2
7	4	9	2	1	3	8	6	5
8	2	6	5	4	7	3	1	9
5	8	2	4	7	1	9	3	6
4	6	3	9	2	8	5	7	1
9	7	1	3	5	6	2	8	4
6	3	7	1	9	5	4	2	8
2	9	8	6	3	4	1	5	7
1	5	4	7	8	2	6	9	3

DOODLE PUZZLE

HalfTime

PAGE 23

Sport Maze

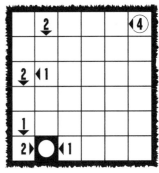

ONE LETTER LESS OR MORE

CABARET

PAGE 24

Checkmate!

M	E	O	W		A	B	B	E	S		A	Q	U	A
A	L	L	I		B	R	U	S	H		N	U	L	L
R	O	A	N		B	I	R	C	H		G	E	N	E
K	I	N	G	C	O	B	R	A		F	L	E	A	S
			N	O	T	E		P	E	R	O	N		
R	E	C	U	R	S		C	A	R	E	S	S	E	D
E	N	A	T	E		B	A	D	G	E		L	E	E
T	E	S	S		M	I	R	E	S		P	A	R	K
A	R	T		B	U	S	T	S		J	A	N	I	E
G	O	L	I	A	T	H	S		F	O	L	D	E	D
		E	R	A	T	O		T	U	B	A			
A	P	R	I	L		P	A	W	N	S	T	A	R	S
B	O	O	T		D	R	U	I	D		I	K	E	A
L	O	C	I		T	I	T	L	E		N	I	P	S
E	L	K	S		S	C	O	L	D		E	N	O	S

PAGE 25

Word Sudoku

N	K	A	O	E	Y	I	S	T
E	O	S	T	I	N	K	A	Y
I	Y	T	S	A	K	E	O	N
Y	I	E	A	S	O	N	T	K
K	A	N	Y	T	E	S	I	O
T	S	O	N	K	I	A	Y	E
S	N	I	K	Y	T	O	E	A
A	T	K	E	O	S	Y	N	I
O	E	Y	I	N	A	T	K	S

SANDWICH
PLANK

PAGE 26

BrainSnack®—Missing Heart

Location 11. Identical cards are always located as far away from each other as the value on the card either horizontally or vertically.

LETTERBLOCKS
BOURBON
TEQUILA

PAGE 27

The Midas Touch

T	H	A	W		P	L	A	C	E		D	O	M	E
R	O	N	A		R	O	B	O	T		A	L	E	G
A	N	O	N		U	R	I	A	H		N	I	N	O
G	O	L	D	E	N	D	E	L	I	C	I	O	U	S
G	R	E	E	C	E			O	L	E				
			R	O	D		P	O	P	U	L	A	T	E
A	N	G	E	L		A	L	A	I			B	O	Y
G	O	L	D	E	N	P	A	R	A	C	H	U	T	E
E	R	I			I	S	I	S		H	A	T	E	D
E	M	B	R	A	C	E	D		R	I	P			
			E	L	K		A	L	P	A	C	A		
G	O	L	D	E	N	R	E	T	R	I	E	V	E	R
E	P	E	E		A	E	R	I	E		N	E	L	L
N	I	N	E		M	A	B	E	L		E	R	I	E
T	E	A	M		E	M	E	R	Y		D	Y	A	N

PAGE 28

Binairo

0	0	1	0	1	1	0	1	1	0	1
0	0	1	0	1	0	1	1	0	1	1
1	1	0	1	0	0	1	0	1	1	0
1	0	1	1	0	1	0	1	1	0	0
0	1	1	0	1	1	0	1	0	0	1
1	1	0	1	1	0	1	0	0	1	0
0	0	1	1	0	1	1	0	1	0	1
1	1	0	0	1	1	0	1	0	1	0
1	1	0	1	0	0	1	0	1	0	1
0	0	1	1	0	1	1	0	1	1	0
1	1	0	0	1	0	0	1	0	1	1

REPOSITION PREPOSITION
WITH RESPECT TO

PAGE 29

Spot the Differences

DOUBLETALK
CONDUCT

PAGE 30

Daddy Ditties

PAGE 31

Cage the Animals

TRANSADDITION
Add S and find RAISES

PAGE 32

Antiquity

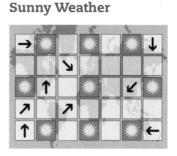

Antiquity generally refers to the period that begins with the introduction of writing.

MISSING LETTER PROVERB
The more the merrier.

PAGE 33

Sunny Weather

BLOCK ANAGRAM
COLLEGE TUITION

PAGE 34

Themeless

C	P	A	S		S	P	E	C	S		S	P	A	S
R	O	L	L		H	I	N	D	U		E	R	L	E
A	L	A	I		I	N	D	I	S	C	R	E	E	T
M	O	R	P	H	E	U	S		P	I	E	C	E	S
		P	U	L	P			H	E	N	N	A		
D	E	P	E	N	D		M	A	N	D	A	R	I	N
O	P	A	R	T		S	A	S	S	Y		I	S	O
T	O	P	S		P	E	N	N	E		C	O	T	S
E	D	E		C	H	E	S	T		B	O	U	L	E
D	E	R	R	I	E	R	E		S	E	N	S	E	S
		M	I	D	A	S		S	W	A	T			
G	L	O	V	E	S		E	L	E	M	E	N	T	S
L	O	N	E	R	A	N	G	E	R		M	O	R	E
I	C	E	R		N	E	G	E	V		P	O	U	R
B	O	Y	S		T	A	S	T	E		T	R	E	E

PAGE 35

Kakuro

1	3	6		3	2	4
5	6		5	9	4	
2	1	6		2		
		9	2	8	3	
6		8	6		5	
9	4	5		3	1	2
7	2			4	9	1

ONE LETTER LESS OR MORE
SURGEON

PAGE 36

BrainSnack®—Curl It

On circle 12. All stones are located diametrically across from an opponent's stone.

END GAME

ENDOCARP
DEFENDED
ENDOZOAN
GENDARME

PAGE 37

Sky Sights

S	T	A	T		S	T	A	L	K		S	P	O	T
A	R	L	O		T	H	R	E	E		C	I	A	O
S	E	E	L		R	E	I	G	N		R	U	H	R
H	E	R	E	C	O	M	E	S	T	H	E	S	U	N
A	S	T	R	I	D	E		U	A	W				
		A	D	E		R	I	C	K	S	H	A	W	
S	L	A	T	E		C	H	O	K	E		A	L	E
N	A	M	E		P	H	O	N	Y		R	A	T	E
U	V	A		M	E	A	D	E		A	E	S	O	P
B	A	N	D	A	N	N	A		T	B	S			
		E	L	K			P	R	I	E	S	T	S	
O	N	C	E	I	N	A	B	L	U	E	M	O	O	N
R	E	A	P		I	S	L	A	M		B	O	N	O
C	A	S	E		F	I	O	N	A		L	E	E	R
A	L	A	R		E	A	T	E	N		E	Y	R	E

PAGE 38

Keep Going

DELETE ONE
Delete T and find ALIBI

PAGE 39

Sudoku

4	9	5	2	1	8	3	6	7
6	3	7	9	5	4	8	2	1
1	8	2	3	7	6	4	5	9
7	2	1	4	3	9	6	8	5
9	5	8	6	2	1	7	3	4
3	6	4	7	8	5	9	1	2
5	7	6	1	4	3	2	9	8
8	4	9	5	6	2	1	7	3
2	1	3	8	9	7	5	4	6

CHANGELINGS

FOUNDATION
SKYSCRAPER
QUADRANGLE

PAGE 40

Movies

B	A	L	I		M	O	L	A	R		D	O	U	R
A	M	I	D		O	P	I	N	E		E	D	G	E
L	O	N	E		R	A	N	D	I		T	O	L	D
M	I	D	N	I	G	H	T	I	N	P	A	R	I	S
			T	R	A			D	O	I				
L	U	C	I	A	N	O		F	E	L	L	O	W	S
O	R	A	T	E		D	A	L	E	Y		B	A	A
G	A	R	Y		R	E	C	U	R		W	E	L	T
I	N	O		L	E	T	T	S		G	I	L	D	A
C	O	M	P	A	S	S		H	E	L	L	I	O	N
			U	Z	I			D	A	D				
C	R	A	Z	Y	S	T	U	P	I	D	L	O	V	E
L	O	D	Z		T	U	N	I	C		I	D	O	L
A	N	I	L		E	N	A	C	T		F	E	L	L
P	A	T	E		D	E	S	K	S		E	A	S	E

PAGE 41

Sport Maze

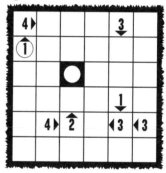

LETTER LINE
UNIVERSITY; VIRTUES, SURVEY, VEINS, TUNERS

PAGE 42

Word Sudoku

D	A	N	T	U	K	E	P	R
U	E	T	R	A	P	D	K	N
K	R	P	E	N	D	A	U	T
P	K	R	A	D	E	T	N	U
E	T	D	U	R	N	K	A	P
N	U	A	K	P	T	R	E	D
T	P	K	N	E	R	U	D	A
A	D	E	P	T	U	N	R	K
R	N	U	D	K	A	P	T	E

ONE LETTER LESS OR MORE
PALMTOP

PAGE 43

BrainSnack®—Fencing

Post 4. A large and a small post always alternate. The number of black posts increases by one from left to right and the number of white posts increases by one from right to left, so it has to be a small white post.

UNCANNY TURN

HAD NO SOLE

PAGE 44

Temperature Extremes

PAGE 45

Cage the Animals

DOODLE PUZZLE

DiscOverIng

PAGE 46

Binairo

I	O	I	I	O	O	I	O	I	O	O	I
O	I	O	I	O	I	O	I	O	I	I	O
O	O	I	O	I	O	I	I	O	I	O	I
I	I	O	O	I	O	I	O	O	I	I	O
O	O	I	I	O	I	O	O	I	O	I	I
I	I	O	O	I	O	O	I	I	O	O	I
O	O	I	O	I	I	O	O	I	O	O
I	I	O	I	O	I	I	O	O	I	O
O	O	I	I	O	O	I	O	O	I
I	O	O	I	I	O	O	I	O	I
O	O	I	O	O	I	I	O	I	O
O	I	I	O	I	I	O	I	O	I

CHANGE ONE

DULL DOWN

PAGE 47

On the Increase

PAGE 48

BrainSnack®—Snow

Group 4. The crystals always link up a short and a long arm. In group 4 they link up two long arms.

BLOCK ANAGRAM

MIDDLE CLASS

PAGE 49

Space Travel

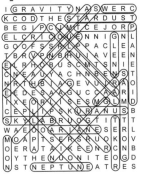

In the beginning of space travel Russia achieved successes, but it was later overtaken by the United States.

FRIENDS

Each can have the PREFIX SHIP- to form a new word.

PAGE 50

Pretty Beat-Up

PAGE 51

Keep Going

REPOSITION PREPOSITION

WITH REGARD TO

PAGE 52

Sudoku

5	7	4	6	2	1	9	3	8
1	3	6	9	7	8	4	2	5
2	9	8	5	4	3	6	1	7
7	5	3	1	8	6	2	4	9
4	2	9	3	5	7	1	8	6
8	6	1	2	9	4	5	7	3
3	4	2	8	6	9	7	5	1
6	8	7	4	1	5	3	9	2
9	1	5	7	3	2	8	6	4

SANDWICH

WIND

PAGE 53

High

LETTERBLOCKS

HIPBONE
JAWBONE

PAGE 54

Word Sudoku

U	M	R	N	T	D	E	A	P
P	N	E	U	M	A	D	R	T
T	D	A	P	E	R	M	N	U
A	U	P	D	R	M	N	T	E
N	T	D	E	A	U	R	P	M
R	E	M	T	N	P	U	D	A
M	P	N	A	D	E	T	U	R
D	R	U	M	P	T	A	E	N
E	A	T	R	U	N	P	M	D

PAGE 55

Sport Maze

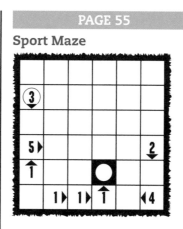

DOUBLETALK

SANCTION

PAGE 56

Low

PAGE 57

BrainSnack®—Honey Cell

Cell 26. Starting from the left and in pairs of columns, columns 1 and 2 each have 1 empty cell; columns 3 and 4 each have 2 empty cells; columns 5 and 6 each have 3 empty cells; columns 7 and 8 each have 4 empty cells; and columns 9 and 10 should each have 5 empty cells.

TRANSADDITION

Add S and find CAREFUL FIRST

PAGE 58

Sudoku Twin

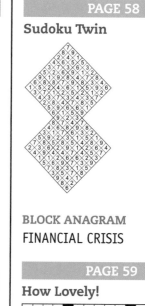

BLOCK ANAGRAM

FINANCIAL CRISIS

PAGE 59

How Lovely!

A	G	A	R		S	H	A	D	Y		F	L	O	W
T	A	L	E		T	E	P	E	E		I	O	T	A
I	B	I	S		A	R	E	N	T		E	V	I	L
L	O	V	E	B	I	R	D		I	N	S	E	C	T
T	R	E	M	O	R			A	T	A				
			B	A	S	I	S		F	R	A	P	P	E
B	A	L	L	S		C	H	A	L	K		P	I	A
O	B	O	E		S	E	A	L	Y		S	L	U	R
S	U	V		C	A	R	L	A		L	O	E	S	S
S	T	E	R	E	O		L	I	L	A	C			
			M	A	D			E	V	A	D	E	D	
P	L	A	T	E	S		L	O	V	E	L	I	F	E
O	A	T	H		I	R	E	N	E		L	O	F	T
O	N	C	E		D	E	V	I	L		E	D	I	E
L	A	H	R		E	D	I	T	S		D	E	E	R

PAGE 60

Sunny Weather

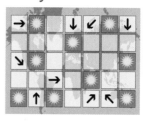

BLOCK ANAGRAM

HURRICANE

PAGE 61

Word Pyramid

C, (1) ac, (2) arc, (3) orca,
(4) roach, (5) choral,
(6) cholera, (7) bachelor

MISSING LETTER PROVERB

All good things must come to
an end.

PAGE 62

Safe Code

48→49→50↓
53←52←51↓

END GAME

C A L E N D A R
P E N D U L U M
S P E N D I N G
V E N D E T T A

PAGE 63

Literary Legends

PAGE 64

Hourglass

(1) tablets, (2) battle,
(3) table, (4) beta, (5) bare,
(6) break, (7) bakers,
(8) bankers

LETTER LINE

HELICOPTER; HOTEL, PILOT,
ELITE, PRICE

PAGE 65

Keep Going

DELETE ONE

Delete I and find JUNIOR
ORCHESTRA

PAGE 66

Twin Openers I

PAGE 67

BrainSnack®—Cookies

Cookie 3. All connections
always depart from a pink
icing cookie.

SQUIRCLES

I C A A C A B I
M A N D O L I N
P M N V O I N G
A E U E K E D O
C L A R I N E T
T S L T E S R S

PAGE 68

Actresses

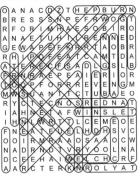

An actress performs in a
theatrical performance or in
a film, on TV or as a cartoon
character.

ONE LETTER LESS OR MORE

ROADBLOCK

PAGE 69

Twin Openers II

PAGE 70

Number Cluster

UNCANNY TURN

HOT WATER

PAGE 71

BrainSnack®—Red Red Wine

Wine label 3. The windows on the top floor of the castle are a different color than the background on all the other wine labels.

DOODLE PUZZLE

CrossCountry

PAGE 72

Punny and Funny I

S	O	S	O		D	R	A	M	A		E	A	C	H
A	M	O	R		R	E	B	U	T		A	G	H	A
R	E	N	D		E	N	A	C	T		G	R	I	N
A	G	A	I	N	S	T	T	H	E	C	L	O	C	K
H	A	R	N	E	S	S				M	O	E		
			A	N	Y		D	E	P	O	S	I	T	S
G	L	A	R	E		T	R	I	T	T		C	O	P
R	O	L	Y		V	E	I	N	S		V	E	R	A
A	G	O		F	I	L	L	E		C	I	D	E	R
M	Y	T	H	I	C	A	L		H	A	S			
			O	A	T		N	O	T	I	C	E	S	
P	O	I	N	T	O	F	N	O	R	E	T	U	R	N
E	A	V	E		R	E	E	L	S		I	R	A	E
A	H	A	S		I	R	A	T	E		N	I	T	A
R	U	N	T		A	N	T	E	S		G	O	O	D

PAGE 73

Sport Maze

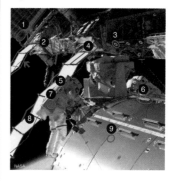

CHANGE ONE

TAKE BACK

PAGE 74

Word Sudoku

M	D	R	L	A	O	E	W	T
O	E	T	W	D	M	R	L	A
A	W	L	R	T	E	D	O	M
R	M	O	T	E	D	W	A	L
L	A	E	M	W	R	O	T	D
D	T	W	O	L	A	M	R	E
E	O	M	A	R	L	T	D	W
T	R	A	D	M	W	L	E	O
W	L	D	E	O	T	A	M	R

LETTERBLOCKS

CYPRESS
HEMLOCK

PAGE 75

Themeless

D	I	N	O		S	O	N	I	C		S	E	L	F
A	D	A	R		A	V	I	S	O		T	A	I	L
C	O	R	N	F	L	A	K	E	S		U	V	E	A
E	S	C	A	L	A	T	E		M	O	D	E	S	T
			M	O	R	E		D	E	N	I	S		
P	A	P	E	R	Y		H	O	T	T	O	D	D	Y
A	L	A	N	A		P	A	T	I	O		R	O	E
T	A	R	T		R	E	B	E	C		R	O	N	A
T	R	A		F	E	T	I	D		P	O	P	E	S
I	M	P	L	I	C	I	T		B	I	S	S	E	T
		H	E	L	O	T		L	U	N	E			
C	A	R	E	E	R		D	I	S	T	A	N	C	E
H	E	A	R		D	I	A	P	H	A	N	O	U	S
E	R	S	E		E	L	L	I	E		N	O	R	M
T	O	E	D		D	E	E	D	S		E	R	B	E

PAGE 76

Sudoku

4	2	6	1	3	7	8	9	5
5	9	1	2	4	8	6	7	3
3	7	8	9	5	6	4	2	1
8	6	2	4	9	3	1	5	7
1	5	3	7	8	2	9	4	6
9	4	7	5	6	1	3	8	2
7	1	4	6	2	9	5	3	8
6	3	5	8	7	4	2	1	9
2	8	9	3	1	5	7	6	4

FRIENDS

Each can have the prefix MAL-to form a new word.

PAGE 77

BrainSnack®—Olives

ABB. For A there is one olive, for B there are two, for C three and for D four. With ABB all possible combinations of groups of two kinds of olives are formed: 1A2B, 1A3C, 1A4D, 2B3C, 2B4D, 3C4D.

SANDWICH

HOUND

PAGE 78

Title Roles

L	E	A	K		A	L	F	I	E		U	S	E	D
E	D	G	E		G	O	O	D	Y		N	A	P	E
G	A	R	Y	C	O	O	P	E	R		A	L	E	E
S	M	A	S	H	U	P	S		E	M	B	L	E	M
			T	A	T			E	L	Y				
M	A	J	O	R	I	T	Y		R	E	E	F	E	R
E	T	O	N	S		H	I	T	I	T		I	R	A
A	S	H	E		C	O	P	E	D		S	E	A	T
T	E	N		L	O	R	E	N		P	U	L	S	E
S	A	N	D	E	D		S	T	R	A	N	D	E	D
		Y	I	N				O	D	D				
M	A	D	E	D	O		B	E	D	R	O	O	M	S
A	R	E	S		P	A	U	L	N	E	W	M	A	N
R	I	P	E		T	H	Y	M	E		N	I	N	O
Y	A	P	S		S	A	S	S	Y		S	T	E	W

PAGE 79

Spot the Differences

LETTERBLOCKS

RUDOLPH
SNOWMAN

PAGE 80

Horoscope

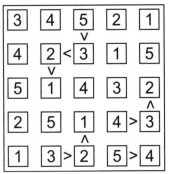

DOUBLETALK

CLIP

PAGE 81

Futoshiki

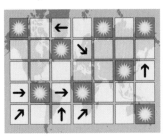

REPOSITION PREPOSITION

IN SPITE OF

PAGE 82

Peewee League

T	A	M	E		T	R	A	M	P		B	O	S	E
O	N	Y	X		R	A	D	I	I		E	L	A	N
A	I	N	U		I	N	A	N	E		F	I	N	D
S	M	A	L	L	T	I	M	E	C	R	O	O	K	S
T	E	S	T	E	E			R	A	G				
		A	G	R	A		O	U	T	S	P	A	N	
C	H	I	N	A		L	O	N	S			A	G	A
L	I	T	T	L	E	B	U	T	T	E	R	C	U	P
A	L	A		T	O	R	O			N	I	T	E	S
P	O	T	S	D	A	M		P	E	N	N			
		A	L	I			D	U	G	O	N	G		
W	E	E	W	I	L	L	I	E	W	I	N	K	I	E
N	A	R	Y		E	E	N	S	Y		E	A	S	E
B	R	I	E		R	E	G	A	N		C	P	A	S
A	P	E	R		S	K	E	I	N		K	I	N	E

PAGE 83

Alpinism

Buildering, usually illegal climbing of the exterior of buildings, is a new, exciting hype.

TRANSADDITION

Add O and find THE RINGS OF SATURN

PAGE 84

Sunny Weather

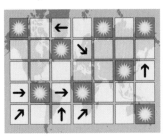

BLOCK ANAGRAM

NEBRASKA

PAGE 85

Punny and Funny II

S	H	E	L		R	E	B	E	C		C	O	I	F
P	A	R	E		A	D	A	N	O		O	L	L	A
A	I	R	S		P	I	N	O	T		F	A	I	R
S	T	O	C	K	I	N	G	S	T	U	F	F	E	R
M	I	R	A	N	D	A			A	R	E			
			Y	E	S		S	U	G	G	E	S	T	S
R	E	N	E	W		L	E	V	E	E		O	O	P
A	V	I	S		S	E	L	E	S		I	N	T	O
M	E	N		S	C	A	L	A		I	N	G	O	T
P	R	O	T	E	I	N	S		A	N	T			
			A	G	E			A	S	C	R	I	B	E
W	A	L	K	O	N	E	G	G	S	H	E	L	L	S
A	L	A	I		C	L	A	R	E		P	O	U	T
Y	A	R	N		E	A	T	E	N		I	N	R	E
S	N	A	G		S	L	E	E	T		D	A	T	E

PAGE 86

BrainSnack®—Write Me

molestie. All words that contain the letters T, O and M are underlined.

END GAME

R E S P L E N D
A P P E N D E D
V E N D I B L E
E N D O G A M Y

PAGE 87

Kakuro

MISSING LETTER PROVERB
Youth is wasted on the young.

PAGE 88

P Soup

P	R	E	P		S	U	M	P	S		S	H	O	W
R	A	V	I		T	R	O	U	T		M	A	L	I
O	N	E	R		A	G	I	L	E		O	D	I	N
P	A	R	A	L	L	E	L	P	A	R	K	I	N	G
			N	I	L				D	O	E			
P	O	S	H	E	S	T		K	I	N	S	M	A	N
I	X	I	A			W	O	O	E	D		A	B	O
P	E	R	S	O	N	A	L	P	R	O	N	O	U	N
E	Y	E		S	O	N	D	E			E	R	S	E
R	E	N	T	I	N	G		K	E	L	P	I	E	S
			A	E	F				L	E	E			
P	O	R	T	R	A	I	T	P	A	I	N	T	E	R
E	R	A	T		T	O	W	I	T		T	I	D	E
R	A	G	E		A	T	O	N	E		H	E	E	D
U	L	A	R		L	A	S	E	D		E	R	N	S

PAGE 89

Word Sudoku

E	N	D	X	T	L	V	S	I
V	X	I	S	E	D	L	N	T
L	S	T	N	V	I	X	E	D
D	T	S	E	L	X	N	I	V
I	E	X	V	N	T	D	L	S
N	V	L	I	D	S	E	T	X
S	L	E	T	X	V	I	D	N
X	I	N	D	S	E	T	V	L
T	D	V	L	I	N	S	X	E

LETTERBLOCKS

WARHOL
CHAGALL

PAGE 90

Keep Going

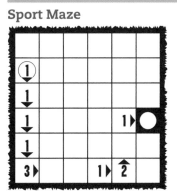

DELETE ONE

Delete T and find OLD MOTHER
HUBBARD

PAGE 91

It's About Time

S	T	L	O		A	L	M	O	S	T		M	A	P
A	R	A	P		R	E	A	D	T	O		I	D	A
S	A	V	E	S	T	H	E	D	A	Y		N	O	T
S	P	A	N	K	E	R	S		L	A	U	G	H	
		M	A	R	S		P	L	A	I	T			
B	U	S	I	L	Y		G	R	A	N	D	E	U	R
E	M	E	N	D		P	O	U	N	D		R	P	I
A	B	C	D		C	H	I	D	E		P	I	T	A
C	R	O		A	L	O	N	E		B	A	C	O	N
H	A	N	D	L	I	N	G		W	E	R	E	N	T
	D	E	C	O	Y		C	O	L	T				
W	A	H	O	O		E	A	R	L	I	E	S	T	
A	R	A		H	O	U	R	G	L	A	S	S	E	S
L	E	N		O	R	A	T	E	D		A	T	T	A
T	A	D		L	O	W	E	R	S		N	E	A	R

PAGE 92

Sport Maze

LETTER LINE

KINGFISHER; GRIEF, HINGE,
FRISK, FEIGN

PAGE 93

Sudoku

7	6	3	4	8	5	1	2	9
4	9	2	3	6	1	5	7	8
1	5	8	9	2	7	3	4	6
5	3	7	1	9	6	2	8	4
2	8	9	7	3	4	6	5	1
6	4	1	8	5	2	9	3	7
3	7	4	2	1	9	8	6	5
9	2	5	6	4	8	7	1	3
8	1	6	5	7	3	4	9	2

CHANGELINGS

C H O P S T I C K S
P E R C O L A T O R
T A B L E S P O O N

PAGE 94

BrainSnack®—History Tour

Castle 6. The historian is only
interested in water fortresses.

ONE LETTER LESS OR MORE

INTENSIVE

PAGE 95

Oxymorons I

T	A	L	C		M	E	L	B	A		S	O	A	P
O	L	I	O		I	M	A	L	L		N	I	C	E
T	A	R	S		R	E	P	E	L		A	S	E	A
	R	E	T	I	R	E	D	W	O	R	K	E	R	S
		U	S	E	R			W	O	E				
S	H	A	M	A	N		S	C	I	S	S	O	R	S
T	O	N	E	R		A	L	A	N	S		C	A	M
A	R	T	S		U	S	I	N	G		Y	E	T	I
I	D	I		O	N	S	E	T		L	E	A	S	T
D	E	C	E	M	B	E	R		P	I	A	N	O	S
	A	N	I			L	E	E	R					
I	N	I	T	I	A	L	R	E	S	U	L	T	S	
D	E	M	I		S	A	I	N	T		I	R	K	S
I	V	A	N		E	L	A	T	E		N	O	U	S
G	A	N	G		D	O	L	O	R		G	N	A	T

PAGE 96

Literature

Literary authors want to con-
vey a message with their texts
in an artistic manner.

UNCANNY TURN

POETRY

PAGE 97

BrainSnack®—Weigh it Up

It's impossible to weigh 4
grams correctly using only one
weighing. All the other weights
are possible. For 1, 2 and 8
grams you can use the weights
on one side of the scale. You
weight the other grams as
follows: 3 g = 1 + 2, 5 g + 1 +
2 = 8, 6 g + 2 = 8, 7 g + 1 = 8,
9 g = 8 + 1, 10 g = 8 + 2.

DOODLE PUZZLE

ThinKing

PAGE 98

Oxymorons II

H	O	O	F		C	A	R	A	T		F	U	L	L
A	N	N	O		A	D	O	B	E		O	B	O	E
G	E	E	R			T	I	A	R	A		R	E	D	S
A	G	R	E	E	T	O	D	I	S	A	G	R	E	E
R	A	S	C	A	L	S			P	R	O			
			A	S	E		S	C	O	O	T	E	R	S
A	N	T	S	Y		S	P	O	O	N		C	A	L
B	A	H	T		C	H	U	R	N		P	O	S	E
A	S	O		F	I	O	R	D		P	U	L	P	Y
S	T	U	D	E	N	T	S		F	U	R			
		E	E	N			C	O	M	P	O	S	E	
S	P	E	C	T	A	T	O	R	S	P	O	R	T	S
A	U	R	A		M	A	R	A	T		S	A	Y	S
I	M	A	N		O	R	A	T	E		E	L	L	E
L	A	S	T		N	A	D	E	R		S	E	E	N

PAGE 99

Wind Instruments

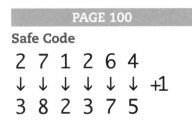

A brass band is an ensemble that consists of brass players and percussion, possibly supplemented with saxophones.

CHANGE ONE
HANDS DOWN

PAGE 100

Safe Code

2 7 1 2 6 4
↓ ↓ ↓ ↓ ↓ ↓   +1
3 8 2 3 7 5

DOODLE PUZZLE
UnEqualLy

PAGE 101

Oxymorons III

S	W	I	M		R	A	C	E	D		P	E	G	S
P	I	S	A		E	M	E	E	R		E	A	R	P
A	D	A	R		C	A	L	L	A		A	R	A	Y
S	E	R	I	O	U	S	L	Y	F	U	N	N	Y	
			E	R	R	S			T	R	U			
S	K	A	T	E	S		M	O	I	S	T	U	R	E
P	A	C	T	S		M	A	G	N	A		T	I	M
A	B	I	E		B	O	U	R	G		P	I	P	E
G	O	D		H	A	L	V	E		A	R	L	E	N
O	B	S	T	A	C	L	E		F	R	I	E	N	D
			H	R	H			S	E	E	N			
	S	T	U	D	E	N	T	T	E	A	C	H	E	R
D	O	R	M		L	O	W	E	D		E	A	V	E
A	C	O	P		O	L	I	V	E		S	L	I	D
S	K	Y	S		R	O	G	E	R		S	O	L	O

PAGE 102

Keep Going

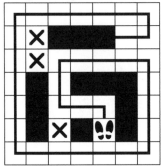

FRIENDS
Each can have the prefix FORE- to form a new word.

PAGE 103

Word Sudoku

I	J	Q	N	T	A	O	S	L
L	S	T	I	O	J	Q	N	A
A	N	O	S	L	Q	T	J	I
Q	T	I	L	N	S	J	A	O
N	O	J	Q	A	I	L	T	S
S	L	A	O	J	T	N	I	Q
O	A	S	J	Q	N	I	L	T
T	Q	N	A	I	L	S	O	J
J	I	L	T	S	O	A	Q	N

SANDWICH
WORD

PAGE 104

Fictional High Schools

S	C	A	M		A	L	O	O	F		M	E	T	E
T	O	R	I		M	I	A	M	I		U	S	E	R
A	L	M	S		I	N	F	E	R		S	A	R	I
B	A	Y	S	I	D	E		N	E	P	T	U	N	E
			P	A	S				W	E	N			
M	A	G	E	N	T	A		C	O	N	T	R	O	L
E	N	O	L			T	H	O	R	N		A	B	A
W	I	L	L	I	A	M	M	C	K	I	N	L	E	Y
L	S	D		L	L	A	M	A			E	L	S	E
S	E	S	S	I	O	N		S	P	R	A	Y	E	R
			C	U	P			O	U	R				
S	H	E	R	M	E	R		L	I	B	E	R	T	Y
N	A	T	O		C	A	B	I	N		A	U	R	A
O	R	A	L		I	N	E	R	T		S	N	O	W
B	E	L	L		A	T	L	A	S		T	E	D	S

PAGE 105

Sport Maze

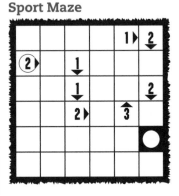

LETTERBLOCKS
MANAGER
PARTNER

PAGE 106

Sudoku X

2	5	9	4	1	8	7	6	3
8	3	6	7	5	2	4	9	1
1	4	7	6	3	9	5	2	8
9	2	3	5	7	4	1	8	6
6	7	4	1	8	3	2	5	9
5	1	8	2	9	6	3	4	7
4	8	1	3	6	5	9	7	2
3	6	2	9	4	7	8	1	5
7	9	5	8	2	1	6	3	4

REPOSITION PREPOSITION
IN PLACE OF

PAGE 107

Wordplay

PAGE 108

BrainSnack®—Symbolism

Symbol 4. Every next figure equals the previous figure where the last piece is a horizontal mirror image and a new piece is added.

DOUBLETALK

BOLT

PAGE 109

Word Pyramid

E, (1) be, (2) bel, (3) able, (4) table, (5) stable, (6) battles, (7) seat belt

TRANSADDITION

Add S and find MAN USES METER

PAGE 110

Sunny Weather

BLOCK ANAGRAM

CELEBRITIES

PAGE 111

More Wordplay

PAGE 112

Sudoku Twin

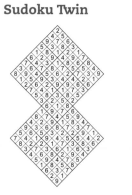

MISSING LETTER PROVERB

All things come to those who wait.

PAGE 113

Futoshiki

END GAME

O F F E N D E D
R E A S C E N D
E N D O R S E E
U N E N D I N G

PAGE 114

Screen Legends Said

PAGE 115

BrainSnack®—Carnival

Vu. Read each word like three sequential letters from right to left.

DOODLE PUZZLE

ZeBra

PAGE 116

The Spy Who Came in From the Cold

7, 13, 1, 23, 2, 26, 11, 15, 5, 4, 16, 20, 30, 27, 18, 6, 8, 3, 12, 10, 19, 28, 9, 29, 22, 25, 24, 17, 21, 14 =

BLU ELE ADE RIS ADO UBL EAG
ENT ARR ANG
ERE NDE ZVO USW ITH BLA CKE
AGL EAN DFO
LLO WCO DET WOT ODI SPO SEO
FPR OBL EMS

BLUE LEADER IS A DOUBLE AGENT ARRANGE RENDEZVOUS WITH BLACK EAGLE AND FOLLOW CODE TWO TO DISPOSE OF PROBLEMS

LETTER LINE

ARCHAEOLOGY; ARGYLE, HOORAY, ORACLE, HEAL

PAGE 117

Presidents Cup—U.S.A.

H	A	A	S		S	H	A	R	P		O	M	I	T
E	T	R	E		T	O	R	A	H		R	I	G	A
A	R	A	L		E	B	O	N	Y		I	C	O	N
T	I	G	E	R	W	O	O	D	S		O	K	R	A
S	P	E	C	I	E	S			I	D	L	E		
			T	E	D		B	A	C	H	E	L	O	R
F	I	D	E	L		A	R	I	A	L		S	L	O
L	O	A	D		S	M	A	L	L		R	O	I	L
A	T	V		E	T	O	N	S		P	E	N	N	Y
G	A	I	N	S	A	I	D		B	E	D			
	D	E	E	M			E	A	R	A	C	H	E	
M	A	T	A		M	A	T	T	K	U	C	H	A	R
A	S	O	R		E	L	I	H	U		T	O	U	R
L	I	M	B		R	U	R	A	L		E	R	T	E
E	A	S	Y		S	I	E	N	A		D	E	E	D

PAGE 118

Keep Going

DELETE ONE
Delete P and find PISTACHIO NUT

PAGE 119

Environment

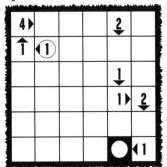

Governments and social organizations attempt to protect the environment.

ONE LETTER LESS OR MORE
AGREEMENT

PAGE 120

Directors Said

A	W	L	S		D	R	A	F	T		E	L	M	S
L	E	E	K		O	I	L	E	R		D	E	M	O
M	L	I	I		O	C	A	L	A		I	N	C	A
A	L	F	R	E	D	H	I	T	C	H	C	O	C	K
		M	A	L			T	O	T					
R	E	C	I	T	E	D		W	O	R	S	H	I	P
A	M	A	S	S		Y	E	A	R	S		O	R	A
M	A	C	H		P	I	L	L	S		S	T	A	G
P	I	T		R	E	N	A	L		S	C	E	N	E
S	L	I	D	I	N	G		S	T	A	R	L	I	T
			I	C	K			R	I	A				
S	T	E	V	E	N	S	P	I	E	L	B	E	R	G
O	H	R	E		I	L	O	N	A		B	R	I	M
H	O	A	R		F	I	E	L	D		L	A	C	E
O	U	S	T		E	M	M	A	S		E	T	O	N

PAGE 121

Sport Maze

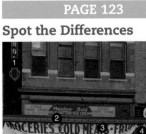

UNCANNY TURN
COUPLES

PAGE 122

Presidents Cup—International

A	P	E	R		A	D	L	I	B		A	G	R	A
P	E	R	I		S	H	I	V	A		F	R	O	M
S	A	I	D		C	O	D	E	D		R	E	D	O
E	R	N	I	E	E	L	S		D		A	G	E	S
			C	I	N	E		S	E	T	I	N		
A	B	S	U	R	D		S	A	L	A	D	O	I	L
M	A	C	L	E		O	P	T	E	D		R	N	A
A	C	H	E		I	N	L	A	Y		S	M	U	G
S	O	W		A	S	I	A	N		B	L	A	R	E
S	N	A	P	S	H	O	T		R	E	I	N	E	R
		R	O	S	I	N		B	A	L	M			
M	I	T	T		K		J	A	S	O	N	D	A	Y
O	O	Z	E		A	S	A	B	C		E	U	R	O
O	W	E	N		W	O	N	K	A		S	P	E	W
S	A	L	T		A	D	E	A	L		S	E	A	L

PAGE 123

Spot the Differences

CHANGE ONE
BLUE JEANS

PAGE 124

Sudoku

1	7	9	3	2	6	4	5	8
6	2	4	5	8	1	9	7	3
8	5	3	4	7	9	6	2	1
3	9	8	6	4	7	2	1	5
2	6	1	9	5	3	8	4	7
7	4	5	8	1	2	3	9	6
4	8	2	7	3	5	1	6	9
9	1	7	2	6	8	5	3	4
5	3	6	1	9	4	7	8	2

SQUIRCLES

```
O L E C E M A A
P Y R A M I D S
T R E N E R V S
I I C V R R E I
O C T A G O N S
N S S S E R T T
```

PAGE 125

Word Sudoku

A	W	I	T	R	D	E	M	L
M	L	R	E	I	W	A	D	T
E	D	T	M	A	L	W	R	I
T	E	W	I	D	R	M	L	A
L	R	D	A	M	T	I	W	E
I	A	M	W	L	E	R	T	D
R	M	L	D	E	A	T	I	W
D	T	A	R	W	I	L	E	M
W	I	E	L	T	M	D	A	R

DOODLE PUZZLE
GrAnt

PAGE 126

BrainSnack®—Outlines

N. All letters that only appear once have a red outline.

UNCANNY TURN
OR HUGE CATS

PAGE 127

Webster Says Not I

PAGE 128

Hourglass

(1) hamster, (2) harems, (3) shame, (4) same, (5) semi, (6) smile, (7) simple, (8) impulse

FRIENDS
Each can have the suffix -LESS to form a new word.

PAGE 129

Horoscope

SANDWICH
SHIP

PAGE 130

Webster Says Not II

R	A	N	C	H		L	E	A	R		M	R	E	D
O	M	A	H	A		O	R	L	E		A	H	S	O
T	A	P	I	R		W	I	L	D		R	E	A	L
C	H	A	N	N	E	L	S		E	N	T	A	I	L
		E	E	L	Y		L	E	A	H				
A	G	A	S	S	I		L	A	M	B	A	S	T	E
L	A	N	E	S		F	A	K	E		S	W	A	B
O	T	I	C		L	I	N	E	R		V	A	N	S
N	O	S	H		I	N	K	S		B	I	N	G	E
G	R	E	E	N	B	A	Y		L	E	N	N	O	N
			C	A	R	L		P	E	L	E			
Y	A	N	K	E	E		S	U	K	I	Y	A	K	I
O	N	C	E		T	H	O	R		N	A	R	I	S
G	N	A	R		T	O	T	E		D	R	A	W	N
I	S	A	S		O	I	S	E		A	D	M	I	T

PAGE 131

Bicycle

Cycling is good for your health, pleasurable and in the city you often reach your destination faster than in a car.

LETTERBLOCKS
OREGANO
PAPRIKA

PAGE 132

The Puzzled Librarian

(1) *A Farewell to Arms*
(2) *Native Son*
(3) *The Hunt for Red October*
(4) *Brideshead Revisited*
(5) *The Satanic Verses*
(6) *The Day of the Locust*
(7) *Finnegans Wake*
(8) *Naked Lunch*
(9) *Watership Down*
(10) *The Lord of the Rings*

REPOSITION PREPOSITION
PURSUANT TO

PAGE 133

Themeless

S	H	E	M		A	S	C	O	T		S	N	O	B
P	A	P	A		L	I	A	N	A		H	O	L	E
A	R	I	T	H	M	E	T	I	C		O	N	E	S
S	E	C	T	I	O	N	S		T	R	U	C	K	S
			E	N	N	A		P	L	A	T	H		
S	A	C	R	E	D		K	E	E	P	S	A	K	E
A	S	H	E	S		C	L	A	S	S		L	I	B
V	I	E	D		P	E	E	K	S		F	A	N	S
O	D	E		D	E	L	I	S		C	O	N	T	E
R	E	S	T	R	A	I	N		M	A	R	T	E	N
			E	R	I	C	A		D	A	R	E		
E	S	C	A	P	E		D	I	R	E	C	T	O	R
S	L	A	V		F	O	R	M	I	D	A	B	L	E
T	A	K	E		U	R	A	L	S		S	A	G	A
O	P	E	L		L	I	B	Y	A		T	R	A	P

PAGE 134

Sport Maze

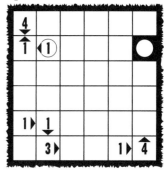

DOUBLETALK
LEFT

PAGE 135

Kakuro

6	1	7	■	1	5	■	3	2
9	2	■	2	9	3	■	4	1
5	3	7	6	■	8	1	■	3
8	■	8	■	■	■	3	5	6
■	9	4	8	■	6	7	4	■
1	5	■	1	7	3	■	1	2
3	2	7	■	2	1	8	■	4
8	■	4	■	6	■	6	7	8
4	2	9	7	■	1	7	8	9

TRANSADDITION

Add A and find STATUE OF LIBERTY

PAGE 136

Homophone Humor

PAGE 137

BrainSnack®—Missing Corner

Cube 3. Look at the cubes in pairs (vertical pairs on left and right sides). On the edge and in the center of each side the colors are repeated in the same order. The same pattern is repeated on the top.

BLOCK ANAGRAM

ENGAGEMENT

PAGE 138

Word Sudoku

E	H	L	U	P	I	R	M	S
I	U	M	L	R	S	P	H	E
R	S	P	M	H	E	L	U	I
U	R	I	H	S	L	M	E	P
M	L	H	I	E	P	S	R	U
P	E	S	R	U	M	H	I	L
S	M	R	E	L	U	I	P	H
L	I	E	P	M	H	U	S	R
H	P	U	S	I	R	E	L	M

UNCANNY TURN

POSTMAN

PAGE 139

BrainSnack®—Number Block

4. In all the other groups the white blocks are located inside the cluster, never at the edge.

END GAME

A S C E N D E D
R E P E T E N D
E N D R U D G E
A T T E N D E E

PAGE 140

More Homophone Humor

O	P	A	L	■	A	R	G	O	N	■	D	A	M	P
R	E	N	O	■	M	O	O	R	E	■	E	R	I	E
A	R	N	O	■	O	P	A	R	T	■	N	O	E	L
D	U	A	L	D	U	E	L	■	W	O	N	O	N	E
■	■	I	A	N	S	■	T	O	L	E	■	■	■	■
A	S	C	E	N	T	■	H	A	R	E	H	A	I	R
B	E	A	U	■	S	M	O	C	K	■	Y	U	M	A
L	A	R	■	I	R	K	■	■	■	R	A	D	■	■
E	T	T	A	■	T	A	N	Y	A	■	S	A	G	A
R	O	A	M	R	O	M	E	■	M	E	T	E	O	R
■	■	■	B	I	B	I	■	M	I	L	E	■	■	■
S	P	A	R	T	A	■	W	E	A	K	W	E	E	K
K	A	T	O	■	C	L	I	M	B	■	A	N	T	I
I	S	I	S	■	C	A	R	O	L	■	R	Y	A	N
M	O	P	E	■	O	B	E	S	E	■	T	O	L	D

PAGE 141

Sudoku X

2	8	4	1	6	9	5	7	3
7	9	5	2	3	4	1	6	8
6	3	1	8	7	5	4	9	2
9	5	6	3	4	8	2	1	7
8	1	3	7	5	2	9	4	6
4	2	7	9	1	6	8	3	5
3	4	2	6	8	1	7	5	9
5	7	9	4	2	3	6	8	1
1	6	8	5	9	7	3	2	4

UNCANNY TURN

THE DAWNING

PAGE 142

Safe Code

96 ← 48 ← 24
              ↑ ×2
03 → 06 → 12

CHANGELINGS

C A S A B L A N C A
G O L D F I N G E R
S T A G E C O A C H

PAGE 143

What's in a Name I

C	H	A	R	■	N	A	I	L	S	■	T	E	S	S
R	O	B	E	■	A	T	R	I	P	■	E	L	L	A
O	P	E	C	■	G	O	T	T	A	■	R	I	O	T
W	I	L	L	I	A	M	■	A	N	D	R	E	W	S
■	■	■	I	N	N	■	■	■	I	O	O	■	■	■
B	R	A	N	D	O	N	■	G	A	B	R	I	E	L
L	A	C	E	Y	■	E	N	U	R	E	■	D	L	I
A	M	O	R	■	W	A	N	E	D	■	J	O	A	N
D	O	R	■	H	I	R	E	S	■	C	O	N	T	E
E	N	N	E	A	D	S	■	S	C	E	N	T	E	D
■	■	■	C	H	E	■	■	■	O	N	A	■	■	■
M	I	C	H	A	E	L	■	M	A	T	T	H	E	W
O	S	L	O	■	Y	O	U	R	S	■	H	O	L	E
A	L	A	E	■	E	G	R	E	T	■	A	W	O	L
T	E	D	S	■	D	E	E	D	S	■	N	E	I	L

PAGE 144

Keep Going

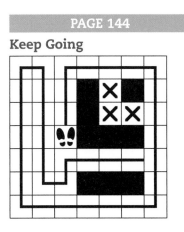

DELETE ONE
Delete D and find MASTERMIND

PAGE 145

Hourglass

(1) federal, (2) feared,
(3) fader, (4) deaf, (5) feud,
(6) Freud, (7) refund,
(8) founder

CHANGE ONE
CLOUD NINE

PAGE 146

What's in a Name II

R O T C	I D A H O	S A L T
O N E A	N A D E R	T R O Y
O M A R	D R A W N	R A N K
M E L A N I E		N A T A L I E
V I A		M E W
B R I A N N A	J E S S I C A
L O R N A	T O O N S	N A G
I S M S	V I S I T	C U R E
N I A	M I L A N	A A R O N
I N S P E C T	T O R R E N T
A N T	R I O
M A D I S O N	L I L L I A N
R O A R	R E G I S	I N T O
E N T E	I T A L O	N O E L
D E A D	A S L A N	E N N A

PAGE 147

BrainSnack®—Recycler

Logo C. Logo A and D are
reversed, B colors are changed,
E and F are warped.

LETTER LINE
PILGRIMAGE; GLEAM, REGAL,
MAGPIE, IMPERIL

PAGE 148

Monkey Business

Peter Pan
Pat the Bunny
Harold and the Purple Crayon
Goodnight Gorilla
Anne of Green Gables

ONE LETTER LESS OR MORE
RELIEVING

PAGE 149

Groaners

PAGE 150

Sport Maze

UNCANNY TURN
FASHION DESIGNER

PAGE 151

Word Sudoku

L	E	H	R	I	T	S	O	X
X	O	I	E	S	H	R	L	T
R	S	T	X	L	O	H	I	E
S	I	E	T	H	X	O	R	L
O	L	R	I	E	S	T	X	H
T	H	X	L	O	R	E	S	I
E	X	S	H	R	L	I	T	O
H	T	O	S	X	I	L	E	R
I	R	L	O	T	E	X	H	S

DOODLE PUZZLE
BreakFast

PAGE 152

Spot the Differences

DELETE ONE
Delete S and find CHAMPAGNE
COCKTAIL

PAGE 153

More Groaners

S S T S	P E T A L	R E S T
A C R O	A M A T I	O P I E
P O E M	S E R I F	L E G S
I N S E C T R E P E L L E N T
D E S T R O Y	T A I
I E R	S T I L E T T O
P L U M E	S C H M O	H A N
I O N E	A U R A E	T E R I
K O I	A R R O W	Y E A S T
A T T A C K E D	A O L
N R A	A L G E B R A
P A S S E N G E R P I G E O N
S L A W	S I T K A	R A V I
I O L E	A N T I C	A N E T
S T A R	S A U N A	M Y R A

PAGE 154

Sudoku X

2	1	7	9	6	8	5	4	3
6	9	4	3	5	2	1	8	7
3	5	8	4	1	7	2	9	6
7	2	5	6	4	9	8	3	1
8	3	9	2	7	1	6	5	4
1	4	6	5	8	3	7	2	9
9	7	1	8	3	5	4	6	2
5	6	2	7	9	4	3	1	8
4	8	3	1	2	6	9	7	5

FRIENDS

Each can have the prefix AUTO-
to form a new word

PAGE 155

Social Contact

By nature, human beings are
inclined to live with sensitivity
for the needs of members of
their society.

SANDWICH

GUARD

PAGE 156

Themeless

C	L	A	W		A	G	A	M	A		S	T	A	T
A	A	R	E		V	A	L	I	D		L	U	N	E
P	R	O	S	C	I	U	T	T	O		A	R	T	E
S	A	N	T	I	A	G	O		R	O	T	T	E	N
			E	T	T	E		B	A	B	E	L		
D	E	C	R	E	E		L	A	B	O	R	E	R	S
E	V	A	N	S		A	I	S	L	E		N	E	W
N	I	T	S		A	L	F	I	E		M	E	N	O
E	T	E		B	L	O	T	S		R	A	C	E	R
B	A	G	P	I	P	E	S		W	I	C	K	E	D
	O	A	T	H	S		R	A	N	K				
C	O	R	N	E	A		N	O	N	S	E	N	S	E
O	L	I	N		B	O	I	S	T	E	R	O	U	S
S	I	Z	E		E	R	N	I	E		E	M	I	T
T	O	E	D		T	R	E	E	D		L	E	T	O

PAGE 157

BrainSnack®—Getting Shirty

Polo shirt 4. All the other polo
shirts have pointed collars.

LETTERBLOCKS

ORGANIC
RECYCLE

PAGE 158

Tennis Players

Tennis originated in England
and has been played in its con-
temporary form since the end
of the nineteenth century.

CHANGE ONE

SLUSH FUND

PAGE 159

9-Letter Isograms

M	A	T	A		A	R	A	B		C	A	N	A	L
I	M	A	M		C	A	L	E		A	L	I	C	E
S	U	N	B	A	T	H	E	R		R	I	G	H	T
E	S	K	I	M	O	S		T	O	R	C	H	E	S
R	E	S	T	E	R		D	O	I	T				
			I	N	S	O		V	I	T	A	M	I	N
A	L	L	O	T		T	O	O	L	S		A	R	E
N	O	U	N		M	A	R	I	E		B	R	I	T
T	L	C		D	O	R	I	C		B	L	E	S	S
A	L	R	E	A	D	Y		E	S	A	U			
		A	R	N	E			P	R	E	C	I	S	
D	E	T	A	I	L	S		G	R	E	N	A	D	E
A	N	I	S	E		P	S	E	U	D	O	N	Y	M
H	O	V	E	L		O	P	E	C		S	O	L	I
S	L	E	D	S		T	A	K	E		E	E	L	S

PAGE 160

Sudoku Twin

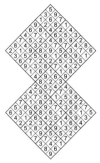

REPOSITION PREPOSITION

INSIDE OF

PAGE 161

Keep Going

DOUBLETALK

WEATHER

PAGE 162

10-Letter Isograms

N	O	D	S		O	R	I	B	I		S	P	E	D
E	L	I	A		R	A	D	O	N		P	A	S	O
R	E	G	U	L	A	T	I	O	N		A	T	M	O
F	A	S	T	E	N	S		M	O	O	C	H	E	R
	E	G	G			C	H	E	F					
B	E	R	R	I	E	S		P	E	R	S	I	S	T
A	R	E	N	T		T	H	A	N	E		N	C	O
N	A	P	E		C	O	U	R	T		A	D	A	R
A	S	U		C	O	I	N	S		S	M	E	L	T
L	E	B	L	A	N	C		E	D	W	A	R	D	S
		L	E	T	S			I	E	R				
O	M	I	N	O	U	S		T	R	A	I	N	E	E
R	I	C	O		M	O	T	H	E	R	L	A	N	D
A	L	A	R		E	T	H	I	C		L	I	O	N
L	A	N	E		R	O	O	S	T		O	L	L	A

PAGE 163

Monkey Business

*Oh, the Places You'll Go
Curious George
In the Night Kitchen
Madeline
How Do Dinosaurs Say Good-night?*

CHANGE ONE

GOOSE BUMPS

PAGE 164

Public Transportation

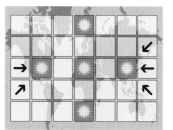

A rickshaw, a kind of bicycle taxi, and a mountable animal can be considered as a form of public transportation.

TRANSADDITION

Add I and find THE RAILROAD TRAIN

PAGE 165

Double Entendres I

D	A	D	O		L	A	B	O	R		S	T	E	R
E	P	I	C		E	T	A	P	E		C	A	M	E
B	A	N	C		S	E	G	A	L		O	L	I	O
T	R	O	U	B	L	E	S	H	O	O	T	E	R	S
		P	O	I				C	H	I				
M	O	R	A	L	E	S		E	A	R	A	C	H	E
U	P	O	N	A		T	A	S	T	E		A	I	N
S	T	A	T		C	E	N	S	E		F	I	N	D
T	I	C		E	L	E	N	A		F	O	R	G	E
S	C	H	O	L	A	R		Y	E	A	R	N	E	D
			T	I	S				N	N	E			
O	R	C	H	E	S	T	R	A	L	S	C	O	R	E
T	E	L	E		I	R	A	N	I		A	N	O	A
T	E	A	R		F	U	N	D	S		S	L	A	V
O	D	D	S		Y	E	A	S	T		T	Y	N	E

PAGE 166

Sunny Weather

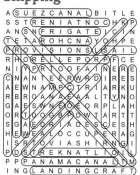

BLOCK ANAGRAM

STATE TROOPER

PAGE 167

BrainSnack®—Pricey Paint

Spray can 4. Replace the symbols with a number from 6 to 1.

END GAME

R E N D I B L E
E N D O Z O I C
E N D E M I S M
F R I E N D E D

PAGE 168

Double Entendres II

L	I	S	P		H	E	A	R	A		U	L	A	N
A	T	T	U		A	R	R	O	W		N	O	N	O
S	C	A	N		P	I	N	T	A		E	N	I	D
S	H	R	I	M	P	C	O	C	K	T	A	I	L	S
			S	E	E			E	O	S				
A	F	G	H	A	N	I		U	N	D	Y	I	N	G
S	L	E	E	T		R	O	M	E	O		D	O	R
C	O	R	D		G	E	L	I	D		B	E	T	A
A	R	M		L	I	N	D	A		S	E	A	R	S
P	A	S	S	A	G	E		K	E	T	T	L	E	S
		O	R	A				L	E	T				
W	I	N	D	I	N	S	T	R	U	M	E	N	T	S
H	O	O	D		T	O	W	E	D		R	A	B	E
O	T	O	E		I	R	A	T	E		E	T	A	L
M	A	N	N		C	A	S	E	D		D	O	R	A

PAGE 169

The Puzzled Librarian

1) *The Gulag Archipelago*
2) *The Adventures of Sherlock Holmes*
3) *The Old Man and the Sea*
4) *The Last of the Mohicans*
5) *Treasure Island*
6) *The Great Gatsby*
7) *Darkness At Noon*
8) *A Town Like Alice*
9) *The Wings of the Dove*
10) *The Maltese Falcon*

MISSING LETTER PROVERB

Love will find a way.

PAGE 170

Shipping

A bit less than ninety percent of international world trade occurs via shipping.

DELETE ONE

Delete B and find EMERGENCY EXIT

Mammals

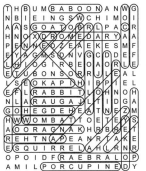

Human beings, chimpanzees and gibbons all belong to the anthropoid family.

MISSING LETTER PROVERB

One volunteer is worth ten pressed men.

Word Pyramid

I, (1) IA, (2) CIA, (3) Inca, (4) manic, (5) iceman, (6) machine, (7) chairmen

LETTER LINE

REVOLUTION; VIOLENT, VIRTUE, UNVEIL, NOVEL

Spot the Differences

DELETE ONE

Delete T and find MANDARIN ORANGES

To the Letter

ANSWERS TO QUICK AND DO YOU KNOW

p 15: Light
p 17: In your throat
p 19: 4
p 21: Atlantic and Pacific
p 23: Snowy
p 25: From algae that, upon dying, turn the Red Sea's intense blue-green water red
p 27: The Sun
p 29: Jules
p 31: Blood
p 33: Albert Einstein
p 35: 5
p 37: Small, steamed cakes made with masa, or ground corn
p 39: Japan
p 41: The science of natural drugs and their physical, botanical and chemical properties
p 43: Nitrogen
p 45: In the eye
p 47: Ethiopia
p 49: *Thunderball*
p 51: Mars
p 53: 6
p 55: In the knee
p 57: China
p 59: Sound effects
p 61: Snoopy
p 63: Some of Scotland's Inner Hebrides islands
p 65: Neptune
p 67: Bumblebee
p 69: The Mad Hatter, the March Hare, the Dormouse and Alice
p 71: The poet Dante
p 73: 5
p 75: Agatha Christie's *Murder on the Orient Express*
p 77: Poopeye, Peepeye, Pupeye and Pipeye
p 79: Victor
p 81: Thermometer
p 83: Pennsylvania Dutch
p 85: A.M. means ante meridiem, Latin for "before noon"; P.M. means post meridiem, Latin for "after noon"
p 87: Charlotte Bronte's *Jane Eyre*
p 89: Piano
p 91: 154
p 93: Earthquakes
p 95: In the stomach
p 97: Petals
p 99: Minesweeper
p 101: Indian
p 103: In the hands (or feet)
p 105: The Andes
p 107: *Brave New World*, by Aldous Huxley
p 109: Charles Lindbergh
p 111: *The Comedy of Errors* (Act III, Scene ii)
p 113: Fat
p 115: Tomato
p 117: Ultra heat treated
p 119: In the brain
p 121: Kim Carnes
p 123: 7
p 125: Argentina
p 127: In the heart
p 129: Apple
p 131: John Wayne
p 133: Grenoble, France
p 135: Port Moresby
p 137: Venezuela
p 139: In the wrist
p 141: Edward Lear
p 143: Samurai
p 145: Someone who won't eat any food of animal origin
p 147: Calla lily
p 149: Butterfly
p 151: Irrawaddy River
p 153: Pinocchio
p 155: Pablo
p 157: A French cheese
p 159: In the pancreas
p 161: Good luck
p 163: 13½" (34 cm)
p 165: 6
p 167: Susan George
p 169: 14
p 171: A horse race
p 173: Noon